TRAUNER VERLAG

GABRIELE RAAB

CHRISTINA KODRÉ

Englisch für die Berufsreife-prüfung – Hauptmodul

■ Forms and Structures – Workbook

Dieses Buch wurde auf Papier aus nachhaltiger Forstwirtschaft gedruckt.

Impressum

Raab u. a., Englisch für die Berufsreifeprüfung – Hauptmodul

■ Forms and Structures – Workbook
2. Auflage 2020, Nachdruck 2022
TRAUNER Verlag, Linz

Die Autorinnen

Mag. Gabriele Raab
Freiberufliche Sprachentrainerin für Erwachsene

Mag. Christina Kodré
Professorin an der HTL Leonding; Abnahme von Externistenprüfungen; Fremdsprachentrainerin für Erwachsene

Dieses Lehrbuch wurde auf der Grundlage des kompetenzbasierten Curriculums Englisch für die Berufsreifeprüfung erstellt und richtet sich nach dem aktuellen Leitfaden für die BRP Englisch; die Auswahl und die Gewichtung der Inhalte erfolgt durch die Lehrenden bzw. Trainerinnen und Trainer.

© 2013
TRAUNER Verlag + Buchservice GmbH,
Köglstraße 14, 4020 Linz
Alle Rechte vorbehalten.

Lektorat/Produktmanagement:
Mag. Katharina Stadler
Korrektorat: Mag. Barbara Altmann
Titelgestaltung: Bettina Victor
Gestaltung und Grafik: Bettina Victor
Schulbuchvergütung/Bildrechte:
© Bildrecht GmbH/Wien
Gesamtherstellung:
Johann Sandler GesmbH & Co KG
Druckereiweg 1, 3671 Marbach

PRINTED IN
AUSTRIA

ISBN 978-3-99062-824-9
www.trauner.at

Vorwort

Das vorliegende Arbeitsbuch **„Forms and Structures – Workbook"** wurde für den Unterricht im **Hauptmodul zur Berufsreifeprüfung** bzw. **Lehre mit Matura aus Englisch** entwickelt. Zusammen mit den Bänden **„Forms and Structures"** und **„Topics"** sowie dem Wortschatztrainer **„Word Power"** dient es der umfassenden Vorbereitung auf die Berufsmatura.

Die Übungen sind wie im Band **„Forms and Structures"** nach grammatischen Schwerpunkten übersichtlich in Kapitel gegliedert, die einzelnen Kapitel sind alphabetisch geordnet.

Sie bieten zusätzlich Übungen, bei denen die Kursteilnehmer/innen die gelernten Inhalte im Kontext anwenden sollen. Diese Texte sind auf die im „Topics"-Band behandelten Themenkreise abgestimmt. Dadurch wird das Gelernte gefestigt und die Anwendung im Kontext ermöglicht. So können bestehende Kenntnisse und Fertigkeiten im Satzbau und in der Grammatik auf dem Niveau B2 erweitert und auf Maturaniveau gebracht werden.

Sollte der letzte Englischunterricht schon einige Jahre zurückliegen, bieten die beiden Bände **„Topics and Language in Use"** und **„Workbook"** des Basismoduls eine optimale Möglichkeit, bereits verblasste Kenntnisse in kurzer Zeit aufzufrischen, verloren Geglaubtes zu aktivieren und wieder mehr Sicherheit im Gebrauch der englischen Sprache zu erlangen. Sie sind bezüglich Themen und Wortschatz auf die Bände des Hauptmoduls abgestimmt und erleichtern den Einstieg.

Das sprachliche Niveau des vorliegenden Bandes entspricht **B2** des Gemeinsamen Europäischen Referenzrahmens für Sprachen (GERS). Die Rechtschreibung orientiert sich grundsätzlich an der modernen britischen Schreibweise.

Zusätzlich für das Hauptmodul erhältlich

- Raab u. a.: Englisch für die Berufsreifeprüfung – Hauptmodul
  - Topics
  A4, broschiert

- Raab u. a.: Englisch für die Berufsreifeprüfung – Hauptmodul
  - Forms and Structures
  A4, broschiert

- Raab: Englisch für die Berufsreifeprüfung – Hauptmodul
  - Wortschatztrainer – Word Power
  A4, broschiert

Die weiteren Bände der „Englisch für die Berufsreifeprüfung"-Reihe

- Raab u. a.: Englisch für die Berufsreifeprüfung – Basismodul
  - Topics and Language in Use
  A4, broschiert

- Raab u. a.: Englisch für die Berufsreifeprüfung – Basismodul
  - Workbook
  A4, broschiert

Wesentliche Elemente und verwendete Symbole

Die angeführten **Ziele** kennzeichnen, über welche **Kompetenzen** die Lernenden nach der Bearbeitung des jeweiligen Kapitels verfügen. Sie orientieren sich am **kompetenzbasierten Curriculum Englisch** für die Berufsreifeprüfung und sind **leitfadenkonform**.

 Meine Ziele

Nach Bearbeitung dieses Kapitels kann ich

- Ziel 1;
- Ziel 2;
- Ziel 3.

Zur Erarbeitung der Kenntnisse und Fertigkeiten sowie zur Kontrolle des Lernerfolgs stehen den Lernenden unterschiedliche **Arbeitsaufgaben** und umfassende **Arbeitsaufträge** („Ziele erreicht?") zur Verfügung, die sich ebenfalls am kompetenzorientierten Curriculum orientieren. Im Mittelpunkt steht hier die **praktische Anwendung** der erarbeiteten Inhalte des jeweiligen Kapitels.

Schriftliche Aufgabenstellungen (Task):

 **Task**

Task 1

Task 2

...

„**Ziele erreicht?**"-Aufgaben am Ende jedes Kapitels zeigen den Kompetenzzuwachs in der Anwendung des Grammatikkapitels auf:

 Ziele erreicht? – Challenge 1/Challenge 2 ...

Folgendes weitere Piktogramm unterstützt das Lehren und Lernen mit dem Buch:

 für Verweise auf andere Bände

STARTEN SIE IHR E-BOOK ZUM BUCH!

 In der TRAUNER-DigiBox (www.trauner-digibox.com) finden Sie Ihr persönliches E-Book zum Buch:

- www.trauner-digibox.com aufrufen
- Einmal kostenlos registrieren
- Ihr E-Book mit **Lizenz-Key** auf der Rückseite des Buches freischalten.

Wir wünschen Ihnen ein spannendes Lernen sowie viel Erfolg beim Anwenden der erworbenen Sprachkompetenzen!

Die Autorinnen

Inhaltsverzeichnis

Starting Off:
The Basic Parts of Speech

Die Wortarten

 Meine Ziele

Nach Bearbeitung dieses Kapitels kann ich

- eine Wortart anhand ihrer Funktion im Satz erkennen;
- Wörter der entsprechenden Wortart zuordnen;
- einige Beispiele für jede Wortart nennen;
- die verschiedenen Wortarten in ihrer Funktion unterscheiden und im Kontext erkennen.

 **Task 1: Structures and Word Function**

Say which part of speech is missing and suggest at least one suitable word.

noun ▪ verb ▪ adjective ▪ article ▪ preposition ▪ present participle (PrP) ▪ past participle (PP) ▪ pronoun

Model sentence:

The royal [_____ noun _____] was born in July.   *baby, prince, heir*

1. Peter is a [_____] boy.

2. Every day I [_____] the newspaper.

3. This is my brother. [_____] name is Ben.

4. There is [_____] book on the desk.

5. In the morning Sue has [_____] for breakfast.

6. This is [_____] American word.

7. I have a pet. It is a [_____].

8. My favourite colour is [_____].

9. The mouse [_____] in the cupboard.

10. This film was really [_____].

11. Sue and Tom were [_____] after the summer holidays.

12. "Hi, [_____] am Betty. What is your name?"

13. At Christmas we always [_____] Christmas carols.

14. The children are having a party. [_____] like parties.

15. The man was sitting in the cafe [_____] a magazine.

16. "This green hat is not [_____]. I have a red one." _____

17. Ralph [_____] apples.

18. Mother wants another cup of [_____]. _____

19. My shoes are [_____]. _____

20. [_____] home Alice met an old friend. _____

21. We have already [_____] our homework. _____

22. Betty saw Jason [_____] to another girl. _____

Task 2: Keywords

The words in the box below are all keywords from the various topics in the book. Write them into the correct columns.

achieve ▪ ambitious ▪ communicate ▪ controversial ▪ dealer ▪ develop ▪ equal ▪ fail ▪ food ▪ global ▪ goods ▪ harmful ▪ impact ▪ increase ▪ language ▪ lethal ▪ media ▪ modern ▪ news ▪ obese ▪ poverty ▪ protect ▪ punish ▪ renewable ▪ separate ▪ smuggle ▪ toxic ▪ treatment ▪ vehicle ▪ vomit ▪ win

Nouns	Verbs	Adjectives

 Ziele erreicht? – Challenge 1: Basic Parts of Speech in Context

First, read the following text.   See 'Topics': Travelling and Tourism

More research on Dark Tourism in the future

'Dark tourism', where visitors travel to sites of death, brutality and terror, is the subject of the world's first centre for academic research, The Institute for Dark Tourism Research at the University of Central Lancashire.

Researchers want to examine why people feel driven to visit sites like Auschwitz or Ground Zero. They look at the relationship between places with terrible associations and tourists who use their leisure time to visit them.

Executive Director Philip Stone says that this includes places such as the site of the 9/11 attacks in New York, Nazi concentration camps and the sites of disasters such as the Chernobyl nuclear accident in Ukraine.

Dr Stone, who worked in the tourism industry before becoming an academic, says his research suggests that visitors want to find some kind of meaning in these places of suffering. They try to identify with the victims and imagine the motivations of the perpetrators. Moreover, visitors have a sense of relief that they can step back into the safety of their own lives. "People feel anxious and uneasy before – and then better when they leave, glad that it is not them," he adds.

His research has looked at people who visit such sites as part of a wider holiday. He describes a couple who reported that they only went to the Ground Zero site at the end of a visit to New York, because going any earlier would have upset them for the rest of the holiday. Nevertheless, they still clearly felt driven to visit the place.

Dr Stone believes that any scene of disaster or violence is going to have an uneasy relationship with tourism – in terms of how sensitively such events are presented, and how visitors are expected to behave. An important part of the attraction of such grim places is to allow people to consider death, from a comfortable distance. In a culture that usually removes death from the public domain, such different places share a common link as scenes strongly associated with the loss of life, he says. "It is a way for a secular society to reconnect with death."

BBC Online – Adapted

perpetrator = person who commits a crime or does something wrong or evil

Now find as many examples for each word class as possible and write them in the correct columns.

Nouns (Singular)		Verbs (Infinitive)		Adjectives

What comes after the Bronze Age and the Iron Age? – The Heavy Metal Age!

Ziele erreicht? – Challenge 2: Present or Past Participle *(-ing or -ed)*

Cross out the wrong words in bold.

See 'Topics': Social Ties

Remember: We use the **past participle** to say how we feel about something:
*She is very **interested** in sports. Younger children feel **bored** quickly when not entertained.*

We use the **present participle** to describe a person or thing that makes us feel in a certain way:
*He is an **interesting** man. This lesson was rather **boring.***

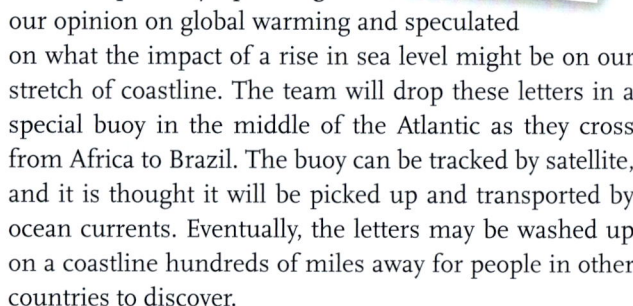

What it is like to be a teenager in the UK I

Global Warming

The more you see or hear about global warming and rising sea levels, the more **desensitised/desensitising** you become – but perhaps it is time to stop and take a look at what they mean. In the next 100 years, Atlantic sea levels are predicted to rise by one-metre. The consequences for people and the environment could be **devastated/devastating**. Many communities will have their lives seriously disrupted, and the coastal landscape may change forever. Some of these changes will be the result of erosion and others the result of the steps **taken/taking** to keep off the sea.

Over the past few months a project **called/calling** Atlantic Rising has been helping students in several schools around Britain and Africa to develop a better understanding of the potential consequences of a one-metre rise in Atlantic sea levels. The team have embarked on a journey around the Atlantic Ocean, **followed/following** the one-metre contour line to document the changes that could occur as a result of the **predicted/predicting** sea level rise.

Before setting off they visited several schools in Britain, including ours, Cardinal Newman Catholic School in Hove. We got involved by following a blog of the expedition and by sending them questions and issues to investigate. We also wrote letters **expressed/expressing** our opinion on global warming and speculated on what the impact of a rise in sea level might be on our stretch of coastline. The team will drop these letters in a special buoy in the middle of the Atlantic as they cross from Africa to Brazil. The buoy can be tracked by satellite, and it is thought it will be picked up and transported by ocean currents. Eventually, the letters may be washed up on a coastline hundreds of miles away for people in other countries to discover.

It may be **reassured/reassuring** for people to know that there are young people around the world who are **concerned/concerning** about the impact of **changed/changing** sea levels and who may have a voice in the future that could bring about change which may reduce its impact. My family and friends are aware of the global warming crisis. By **done/doing** small things such as cycling to the park, taking the bus to town and switching off electrical appliances at home, we are making a contribution towards **reduced/reducing** the greenhouse gases in the atmosphere which could help to reduce global warming. If everybody made small changes to their lifestyles, the impact could be significant.

BBC Online – Adapted
By Kitty from Hove, Brighton, UK

Self-Check

✓ started   ✓✓ on my way   ✓✓✓ accomplished

	✓	✓✓	✓✓✓
I can name and classify the different parts of speech.			
I can give examples for each word class.			
I can use the parts of speech in a sentence correctly according to their function.			
I can distinguish between the various classes of words in context.			

Adjectives and Adverbs

Eigenschafts- und Umstandswörter

 Meine Ziele

Nach Bearbeitung dieses Kapitels kann ich

■ Eigenschaftswörter und Umstandswörter im Gebrauch unterscheiden;

■ die Steigerungsformen richtig bilden und Besonderheiten berücksichtigen;

■ die verschiedenen Möglichkeiten des Vergleichens anwenden.

 **Task 1: Adjective or Adverb**

Fill in the correct forms of the words in brackets.

1. When she was a teenager Ann was an _____ (extreme) _____ (good) tennis
   player. _____ (Unfortunate), she broke her ankle some years ago. Since then she has not been
   able to play tennis at a _____ (high) level any more.

2. "This door lock can be opened _____ (easy) by a burglar. I advise you to buy a
   _____ (new) one", a security agent _____ (recent) told me.

3. "It is _____ (miserable) weather today: it is _____ (cold) and
   _____ (windy). And above all, it started snowing _____ (heavy) some
   minutes ago. So, please, Peter, drive _____ (real) _____ (careful)!"

4. The lorry driver was _____ (serious) injured when he bumped into the tree.

5. As Kevin is _____ (extreme) _____ (clever) his mother is quite
   _____ (proud) of him. Last week he did very _____ (good) in the
   _____ (difficult) Chemistry test as he _____ (near) made no mistake and
   could obviously answer all the questions _____ (easy).

6. He _____ (near) always behaves _____ (confident).

7. My old car broke down yesterday. I hope it can be mended _____ (cheap).

8. Jimmy has got a _____ (tremendous) collection of stones.

9. I am a fan of Pink. She not only sings _____ (excellent), she has got _____
   (outstanding) songs as well.

10. Although he brought the _____ (bad) news to her _____ (gentle), Alice burst
    into tears immediately.

11. Hmmm! The roast beef tastes _____ (delicious). You are a _____ (pretty) _____ (good) cook, Sam! You have never told me that you can cook so _____ (good)."

12. The customs officer looked _____ (careful) at the signature.

13. Have you ever been _____ (wrong) accused of something?

14. "My brother is an _____ (incredible) _____ (successful) businessman", he said _____ (cynical), "He's just gone bankrupt for the fifth time!"

15. The university professor told his students that he would not be _____ (easy) satisfied because his expectations are _____ (usual) _____ (extraordinary) _____ (high).

16. "Have you seen John _____ (late)?" – "Yes, of course. I _____ (near) see him every day. I live _____ (near) to John, only five minutes away."

17. Last week Betty was working _____ (real) _____ (hard) for her presentation. She _____ (hard) took a break. But it was worth the effort: she did an _____ (excellent) presentation and could answer all the _____ (difficult) questions. Betty got an _____ (incredible) _____ (good) feedback from the examiners. She _____ (final) got an A+.

18. Jason told the police that he could not remember the accident very _____ (clear).

19. Granny cannot carry _____ (heavy) things anymore. So she _____ (polite) asked her grandson to help her.

20. "Tom, your performance has become _____ (considerable) _____ (good) _____ (recent)", the teacher said _____ (friendly).

21. "Jason, believe me, this dish tastes _____ (excellent)!"

22. The dog barked _____ (fierce) at the stranger.

23. The number of visitors to the exhibition rose _____ (steep) in the first few months. _____ (Surprising), the number dropped _____ (considerable) last week.

24. A new study shows women are _____ (increasing) becoming their families' principal breadwinners.

25. We are in a _____ (huge) global economy where something that happens in one area can have knock-on effects worldwide. This process is called globalisation. The world is becoming _____ (increasing) interconnected as a result of _____ (massive) increased trade and _____ (cultural) exchange. Globalisation has increased the production of goods and services. Globalisation has been taking place for hundreds of years, but it has speeded up _____ (enormous) over the last half-century.

26. The _____ (tropical) rainforest is an ecosystem with a _____ (constant) temperature and a _____ (high) rainfall. The level of humidity and density of the vegetation provide a _____ (unique) water and _____ (nutrient) cycle.

27. The rainforest nutrient cycle is _____ (rapid). The _____ (hot), _____ (damp) conditions on the forest floor allow for the decomposition of dead plant material. This provides _____ (plentiful) nutrients that are _____ (easy) absorbed by plant roots. However, as these nutrients are in _____ (high) demand from the rainforest's many fast-growing plants, they do not remain in the soil for long and stay close to the surface of the soil. If vegetation is removed, the soils _____ (quick) become _____ (infertile) and _____ (vulnerable) to erosion.

28. Ecotourism encourages visitors to a country to leave a _____ (small) carbon footprint to the benefit of _____ (local) communities and environments. It has become an _____ (increasing) _____ (popular) option for many people. Ecotourism is a type of _____ (sustainable) development. Its aim is to reduce the impact that tourism has on _____ (natural) _____ (beautiful) environments.

29. In the last _____ (few) years, many businesses have been very _____ (successful). They have produced a lot of _____ (new) products and developed _____ (new) technologies. _____ (Unfortunate), many of the businesses that are established every year, more than a third, do not survive the first years. So well-planned marketing and advertising strategies are key to running a business _____ (successful).

30. The family in Britain is changing. The once _____ (typical) British family headed by two parents has undergone _____ (substantial) changes during the twentieth century. In particular, there has been a rise in the number of single-person households, which increased from 18 to 29 per cent of all households between 1971 and 2002. By the year 2030, it is estimated that there will be more _____ (single) people than married people. Fifty years ago this would have been _____ (social) _____ (unacceptable) in Britain. In the past, people got married and stayed married. Divorce was very _____ (difficult) and _____ (expensive) and took a _____ (long) time. Today, people's views on marriage have changed. Many couples live together without getting married. Only about 60 % of these couples _____ (eventual) get married.

vulnerable = anfällig

A small, thin man walked into a pub and shouted angrily,
"Who has painted my car bright purple?"
A huge man with big muscles got up and said frighteningly, "I did".
"Oh," said the small man, "I thought I'd let you know that the first coat is dry."

coat = hier: Schicht

Task 2: Adjective or Adverb and Comparison

Fill in the correct forms of the words in brackets.

1. Father has been very busy _____ (late).

2. The pupils could have done this test _____ (easy) with a computer.

3. Sue is always _____ (good) dressed. She always follows the _____ (late) fashion.

4. People should exercise _____ (often). Otherwise they could put on weight _____ (easy).

5. The _____ (near) train leaves in five minutes.

6. If there are any _____ (far) questions, please do not hesitate

7. It cost _____ (little) money than I expected.

8. The film was _____ (exciting) than the book.

9. 'Origin' is Dan Brown's _____ (late) novel. I hope this won't be his _____ (late).

10. This is the _____ (interesting) project I have ever done.

11. The child tasted the soup _____ (careful).

12. Who made the _____ (few) mistakes?

13. The patient slept _____ (bad), even _____ (bad) than the night before.

14. Patrick has attended classes _____ (regular) and now he can speak Spanish _____ (real) _____ (fluent). Sometimes it is not _____ (easy) to understand him because he speaks so _____ (terrible) _____ (fast). His pronunciation is _____ (good). He can pronounce _____ (near) all the words _____ (correct).

15. Mother _____ (normal) is _____ (patient) than father.

16. This is the _____ (late) news for today.

17. These days it is becoming _____ (hard) and _____ (hard) for teenagers to find a _____ (good)-paid job.

18. I thought that the tickets would be rather _____ (expensive) but they were _____ (reasonable) _____ (cheap).

19. Our holiday was too _____ (short). Time passed _____ (quick).

20. As I got up _____ (late) that morning, I only had a _____ (quick) shower and no breakfast.

21. Sarah was rather _____ (unfriendly) to me at the party. She _____ (hard) spoke to me. I was _____ (real) surprised because _____ (normal) she greets me _____ (friendly) and _____ (near) always stops to talk to me _____ (polite).

22. The _____ (tropical) rainforest biome is found in _____ (hot), _____ (humid) environments in equatorial climates. They contain a _____ (diverse) range and the _____ (high) volume of plant and animal life found anywhere on earth.

23. In general, _____ (tropical) rainforests have _____ (hot) and _____ (humid) climates where it rains _____ (virtual) every day. The level of rainfall depends on the time of

year. Temperatures vary through the year – but much _____ (little) than the rainfall. The rainy season

is from December to May: the _____ (high) monthly rainfall is in March with over 300 mm, while it is

_____ (low) is in August with _____ (little) than 50 mm. Over the year, the temperature

only varies by 2°C.

24. Tourism is a _____ (rapid) growing industry and has a far-reaching _____

(economic) and _____ (environmental) impact across the world. In 2019, 940 million

people were recorded as having arrived in a country from abroad because of tourism. This is worth 919 billion dollars,

making tourism one of the world's _____ (large) industries.

25. Tourism is also one of the world's _____ (fast) growing industries. In 2019, the Middle East and Asia

had the _____ (great) growth of tourists. Europe still has the _____ (great) number of

tourists – _____ (near) 500 million in 2019. The tourism industry therefore is very _____

(important) to _____ (economic) growth as well as the environment.

As countries develop and consumption increases so does the amount of waste per capita, and pollution becomes a

_____ (great) problem. There are _____ (global) as well as _____ (national)

and _____ (local) strategies in place to reduce levels of waste and minimise impact on the environment.

27. The amount and type of waste produced varies between countries. MEDCs have _____ (high) levels of

consumption, so many produce _____ (much) waste than LEDCs. Ireland and the USA produce over

700 kg of waste per person per year. In LEDCs the figure is around 150 kg per person per year. This difference is due to

_____ (different) levels of consumption; it is also _____ (common) to reuse

items in LEDCs.

28. As a country becomes _____ (wealthy), the demand for consumer items increases. This means that

items are replaced _____ (frequent) – leading to _____ (large) quantities of waste. For

example, mobile phones and computers that still work may be thrown away for a _____ (new) version.

29. In LEDCs waste production is _____ (low) because _____ (little) is bought as people have

a _____ (low) income, and _____ (little) packaging is used on products.

30. A _____ (new) study shows that women are _____ (increasing) becoming

their families' principal breadwinners: many of these women are _____ (single) mothers struggling

to make ends meet. But the news is not _____ (exact) _____ (rosy) for married women

who are _____ (good) paid. According to economists from the University of Chicago School of Business,

couples in which the wife earns _____ (much) than her husband report being _____ (little)

happy with their marriage and have _____ (high) rates of divorce.

per capita = pro Kopf
to make ends meet = über die Runden kommen

"I thought you weren't going to smoke any more." – "I'm not."
"But you are smoking as much as ever." – "Well, that's not more, is it?"

Ziele erreicht? – Challenge 1: Adjective or Adverb

Fill in the correct forms of the words in brackets.

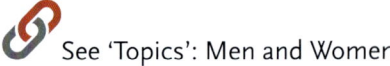 See 'Topics': Men and Women

Men not expected to do more housework in the future

Household chores are a frequent source of domestic disputes between lethargic husbands and their _____ (hard-working) wives, but women have been warned not to expect men to pull their weight any time soon.

A _____ (recent) study from Oxford University has found that men are unlikely to be doing an _____ (equal) share of the vacuuming, dusting and washing up much before 2050. Mothers, the researchers warned, will continue to shoulder the burden of childcare and housework for the next three decades, _____ (main) because routine chores such as cleaning and cooking are still regarded as "women's work". The gap between the amount of time men and women spend on housework has narrowed _____ (steady) over the past 40 years.

Nevertheless, if _____ (current) trends continue, it will take another three decades before true domestic equality is achieved, the study concluded. Academics at Oxford's Centre for Time Use Research analysed 348,000 diary entries, in which men and women recorded how much time they spent on housework and childcare each day. The survey was completed by people aged between 20 and 59 in the UK and 15 other industrialised countries, including Norway, Denmark, the USA, Australia, and France.

The research suggested that across the group, including in Britain, societies are in the middle of a 70–80 year process towards equality in housework and caring for children. In the Nordic countries, the burden of housework is shared more _____ (equal) between men and women, the academics found. In the UK, however, women spend an average of four hours and 40 minutes each day on domestic chores and childcare duties, compared with two hours and 28 minutes for men. This was an improvement from the 1960s, when British women _____ (typical) spent six hours a day on housework, while men contributed just 90 minutes of their time every day.

However, in some countries progress towards domestic equality appears to be going rather _____ (slow), the report found. Dr Oriel Sullivan, a research reader from Oxford's Department of Sociology, said many routine chores such as cooking, cleaning, and looking after children are still _____ (wide) seen as 'women's work'. Men, however, continue to dominate 'masculine' domestic jobs, such as DIY, car maintenance and work outside the house. "We have looked at what is stopping equality in the home, and we have found that certain tasks seem to be allocated according to whether they are viewed as men's or women's work," she said.

Dr Sullivan said _____ (cultural) attitudes, reinforced at school, may be responsible for still existing traditional gender-specific views of _____ (different) domestic jobs. "At school it is much easier for a girl to be a Tom-boy, but it is much more _____ (difficult) for a boy to enjoy baking and dancing because he will be defined as a 'sissy' ", she said.

The research also found that social policies affect the division of labour at home. Men and women share housework more _____ (equal) in Nordic countries which offer parents more balanced maternity and paternity leave and provide more state childcare services. These countries regard women as full members of the workforce and not _____ (primary) mothers and "home-makers", the researchers said.

THE TELEGRAPH – ADAPTED

to pull one's weight = seinen Teil beitragen   sissy = das 'Weichei'

Ziele erreicht? – Challenge 2: Adjective – Comparison

Fill in the correct forms of the words in brackets (+big = bigger; ++big = biggest).

See 'Topics': Learning and Education

How much can children learn at Key Stage 1?

The world of a five-year-old is about to get a whole lot _____ (+demanding) thanks to the introduction of a new national curriculum. But how much can a five-year-old realistically learn?

As every teacher will tell you, children's development in the five to seven age group, known as Key Stage 1, is elastic. Parents are constantly reassured that youngsters learn at different rates and at different speeds. Critics fear that making things _____ (+tough) at an early stage could be a counterproductive move, as children who do not progress so fast may feel that they are failing.

Primary education specialist John Coe says the notion that learning _____ (+much) at an earlier stage makes _____ (+good) results is not supported by academic research. The veteran head teacher, and spokesman for the National Association for Primary Education says: "Professionals and academics agree that this is _____ (+great) than the personal and developmental capacity of children who are five and six years old. Young children learn through their own direct experience, through things in which they are involved, that happen to them in a multi-sensory way – their touch, their sight, their sense of smell. Experience is the _____ (++great) teacher of the young." It is only as they mature, he says, that they are able – with the help of skilled educators – to connect learning experiences into ideas that they can hold in their minds.

Primary education expert Jean Gross says: "People think that _____ (++many) children come to school ready-cooked at five, that they have developed the basics. However, for a large proportion of children in this country that is just not the case. Children need continued work in schools to develop the skills of speaking and writing, managing their feelings and developing their social skills and getting on with others. It's much _____ (+important) for children to be learning these skills than to be absorbing facts or reading aloud in class. It is going to be really difficult with summer-born children and those with special educational needs."

Dr Terry Wrigley is a key coordinator of an academics' open letter of opposition to the proposals sent to Michael Gove earlier in the year. He says, "Many five-year-olds will struggle to name 3D shapes or 'instantly' subtract seven from 16," he says. "It is unrealistic to expect children to calculate 5/7 + 1/7 = 6/7 by the age of seven. Can we expect _____ (++many) five-year-olds to spell Tuesday and Wednesday correctly, or six-year-olds to spell 'national' or 'merriment'? Young children are becoming _____ (+skilled) at using technology, but how many 5–7-year-olds will be able to learn how to 'create and debug simple programs'?"

BBC ONLINE – ADAPTED

Self-Check

✓ started ✓✓ on my way ✓✓✓ accomplished	✓	✓✓	✓✓✓
I can use adjectives and adverbs correctly in sentences.			
I can compare two or more people and objects with each other.			
I can use adjectives and adverbs and their comparative and superlative forms appropriately in context.			

Conditional Clauses

 Die Bedingungssätze ('If-Sätze')

 **Meine Ziele**

Nach Bearbeitung dieses Kapitels kann ich

- die vier verschiedenen Grundformen der *If*-Sätze unterscheiden und erkennen;
- die passenden Verbformen bilden und in Bedingungssätzen anwenden;
- selbständig *If*-Sätze richtig bilden und verwenden.

Task 1: Conditional Clauses 'Types 0 and 1'

Fill in the correct form of the words in brackets.

1. If you _____ (press) the button, the computer _____ (start) up.

2. If we _____ (not, deal) with global warming, temperatures _____ (rise).

3. We _____ (catch) the train if we _____ (hurry) up.

4. Sue and Ann _____ (buy) concert tickets if they _____ (not, be) too expensive.

5. Unless you _____ (study) more, you _____ (not, pass) your driving test.

6. _____ (you, tell) him the news if you _____ (see) him?

7. If you _____ (not, know) the word, _____ (ask) your teacher or
_____ (look) it up in a dictionary.

8. We _____ (can) slow down global warming if we _____ (start) reducing our energy
consumption.

9. Water _____ (boil) if you _____ (heat) it to 100° C.

10. If you _____ (freeze) water, it _____ (expand).

11. Ben and Alan _____ (go) swimming if the weather _____ (be) fine.

12. If we _____ (ask) them, they _____ (lend) us their car, I am sure.

13. What _____ (you, do) if you _____ (not, get) the job?

14. If the sea level _____ (continue) to rise, many coastal areas _____ (be) flooded.

15. The students _____ (have) no problems in the test if they _____ (read) through
these texts carefully.

16. If Tom _____ (not, call) his mother, she _____ (get) worried.

17. If you _____ (go) to the festival, you _____ (have) to take a rain coat and rubber
boots with you.

18. If you _____ (move) to Australia, you _____ (must) speak English.

19. If you _____ (read) the manual carefully, you _____ (can) get the device going.

20. People _____ (become) quite old if they _____ (do) sports regularly.

 **Task 2: Conditional Clauses 'Type 2'**

Fill in the correct form of the words in brackets.

1. If I _____ (be) a famous musician, I _____ (move) to Los Angeles.

2. I _____ (not, do) that if I _____ (be) you.

3. There _____ (be) less air pollution if people _____ (use) public transport regularly.

4. If everyone _____ (recycle) paper, metal and glass, we _____ (not, produce) so much rubbish.

5. If Peter _____ (work) less, he _____ (enjoy) life more.

6. You were quite rude to Jill. I _____ (apologise) if I _____ (be) you.

7. If Shakespeare _____ (be) alive today, what _____ (he, write) about?

8. They _____ (stay) at home if it _____ (rain).

9. My parents _____ (be) pleased if you _____ (come) to the party.

10. David said that he _____ (risk) losing all the money if he _____ (be) you.

11. Jason _____ (buy) a new car if he _____ (get) much money for the old one.

12. If Aaron still _____ (have) his villa in Italy, we _____ (can) spend some days there. It is a pity that he sold it last year.

13. If Sue _____ (get) better marks at school, she _____ (be) allowed to go to the festival in June.

14. What _____ (you, do) if you _____ (win) in the lottery?

15. Ann _____ (go) out more often if her parents _____ (not, be) so strict.

16. If I _____ (be) you, I _____ (talk) to her openly.

17. I _____ (protect) my private life if I _____ (become) a famous star.

18. You _____ (not, cough) so much if you _____ (not, smoke).

19. "If that mountain bike _____ (not, be) so expensive, I _____ (buy) it." – "Well, if I _____ (be) you, I _____ (take) on an odd job."

20. "Hmmm! This chocolate cake tastes delicious! If you _____ (sell) them, you _____ (make) a fortune."

Scientist: "This gas is a deadly poison. What steps would you take if it escaped?"
Student: "Large ones, sir!"

Task 3: Conditional Clauses 'Type 3'

Fill in the correct form of the words in brackets.

1. What _____ (Tom, do) if his boss _____ (not, agree) to give him
   a pay rise?

2. If you _____ (not, drink) so much alcohol at the party yesterday, you
   _____ (feel) better now.

3. "Great! We've run out of petrol! If you _____ (listen) to me instead of being
   so stubborn, you _____ (hear) me saying that we were getting low. Then we
   _____ (not, be) stuck here!"

4. If Kate Middleton _____ (not, go) to St. Andrews University in Scotland, she
   _____ (not, meet) Prince William.

5. "We are lost! If we _____ (bring) the map with us, we _____
   (know) where we are."

6. Tim was lucky to discover the fire in time. If he _____ (not, install) a smoke detector, the
   house _____ (burn) down.

7. What _____ (happen) if the lifeguard _____ (not, be) there?

8. If Betty _____ (talk) to her parents openly, they _____ (not, be)
   so angry now.

9. Unfortunately, the concert was sold out within a few hours. However, if I _____ (get)
   tickets, I _____ (go) to the concert.

10. If Alice _____ (live) a healthier life, she _____ (not, be) obese
    now.

11. If Tim _____ (not, be) so self-centred, his wife _____ (not,
    leave) him.

12. Ann _____ (not, be) late if she _____ (set) her alarm clock
    yesterday evening.

13. If it _____ (not, be) so hot, there _____ (not, be) so many bush
    fires now.

14. What _____ (you, do) if you _____ (get) the job?

15. If Alan _____ (not, be) so nervous, he _____ (pass) the exam.

16. If Nick _____ (get) up in time, he _____ (catch) the train. So he
    _____ (not, be) late for the meeting.

17. If Sue _____ (get) better marks at school, she _____ (be)
    allowed to go to the festival last weekend.

18. If granddad _____ (work) less, he _____ (enjoy) life more.

19. Jason _____ (still, be) alive if he _____ (be) more careful.

20. Mark _____ (not, suffer) from lung cancer now if _____ (not,

smoke) so much the last 30 years.

 **Task 4: Conditional Clauses – Mixed Types**

Fill in the correct form of the words in brackets.

1. If it _____ (rain), I will stay at home.

2. If you heat a piece of metal, it _____ (expand).

3. If mother were here, she _____ (know) what to do.

4. The students _____ (succeed) if they had studied harder.

5. If Alice had lived a healthier life, she _____ (put) on so much weight. She
_____ (not, be) obese now and _____
(can enjoy) life more.

6. If the burglar had come through the garden, he _____ (leave) some footprints.

7. If Paul _____ (not, eat) that much, he would not have stomach ache now.

8. Mother would be glad if you _____ (help) her with the housework.

9. Alice and Susan _____ (go) to the party if they had been invited.

10. If women did not take on the burden of domestic duties, they _____ (can
work) the long hours needed to win top jobs.

11. If Mary does not take her umbrella, she _____ (get) wet.

12. Alice might have avoided the mistake if she _____ (be) more careful.

13. Mr Smith would have stayed if his boss _____ (give) him a pay rise.

14. If everyone recycled paper, glass and metal, we _____ (not, produce) so much
waste.

15. We _____ (be) disappointed if there had been no snow in the mountains.

16. If Macy knew everything about his life, _____ (still, she, love) him?

17. Tom _____ (not, be) allowed to go to the festival in June if he does not get
better marks at school.

18. If father _____ (know) him before, he would not have allowed his daughter Jill
to marry him.

19. If George had got up in time, he _____ (not, have) to hurry now.

20. If Paul _____ (give) up smoking, would he have a chance?

21. I _____ (not, swim) in this dirty river if I were you.

22. If Mr Gomez, the Spanish teacher, had not spoken so fast, the students _____
(can understand) him.

23. What _____ (you, do) if the bus had not come in time?

24. If you leave now, you _____ (get) there in time.

25. What would happen if I _____ (open) the door?

26. If Jason had told Betty the truth, she _____ (not, leave) him.

27. If I were you, I _____ (give) up smoking at once.

28. The children _____ (cannot) go out unless it stops raining.

29. If Tom had been more careful, he _____ (not, have) that accident. He _____ (not, be) in hospital now.

30. If you were a millionaire, what _____ (you, do)?

31. If the pilot had made a mistake, the plane _____ (crash).

32. If the children had not changed their wet clothes, they _____ (catch) a cold.

33. If you _____ (not, turn) the radio down, I will go mad!

34. If my brother were here, he _____ (help) us now.

35. We _____ (can ask) him for help if we had known his telephone number.

36. What _____ (you, do) if a burglar entered your house?

37. If you put water into the freezer, it _____ (freeze).

38. If Phil had more time, he _____ (spend) every Sunday in the mountains.

39. If Nick trains regularly, his performance _____ (improve).

40. You _____ (understand) what I mean if you read my letter carefully.

Mother: "If you eat any more of this pie, you will burst."
Little Jane: "Okay, Mum – just pass the pie and get out of the way."

🎯 **Ziele erreicht? – Challenge 1: Conditional Clauses 'Type 1' – Lose weight: What happens if ...**

Form if-clauses according to the model sentence.

Model sentence: eat less meat → lose weight immediately
If you eat less meat, you will lose weight immediately.

1. keep a food journal → realise how much food you actually consume all day.

_____

_____

2. choose water instead of sugary drinks → feel less thirsty

_____

3. take smaller portions → eat much less

4. not skip breakfast in the morning → can concentrate better at work

5. have at least five servings of fruit and vegetables a day → easily get enough vitamins

6. eat fewer sweets → consume much fewer calories

7. read nutrition labels more carefully → find out quickly which products are high in fat and sugar

8. exercise regularly → get in better shape soon

Now add some further sentences yourself.

9.

10.

11.

12.

🎯 **Ziele erreicht? – Challenge 2: Conditional Clauses 'Type 2' – Environment: What would happen ...**

Form if-clauses according to the model sentence.

Model sentence: everybody, drive more slowly → the air, be less polluted
If everybody drove more slowly, the air would be less polluted.

1. car companies, produce cheaper electric cars → a lot of people, buy one

2. people, eat less meat → farmers, keep fewer cows and pigs

3. we, wear more fair trade clothes → female workers in Bangladesh, earn more money

4. we, not consume so many burgers → fast food companies, not destroy so much land

5. everybody, go to work by bike or by train → we reduce our carbon footprint dramatically

6. nobody, buy products made from tropical woods → we, can save the rainforests

7. we, throw away fewer plastic bags → the oceans, are less polluted.

8. less water, is used for golf courses in hot areas → farmers, can water their fields.

Now add some further sentences yourself.

9.

10.

11.

12.

🎯 **Ziele erreicht? – Challenge 3: Conditional Clauses 'Type 3' – History: What would have happened …**

Form if-clauses according to the model sentence.

Model sentence: Austrian Empress Elizabeth not be such a beauty → people, not love her so much
If the Austrian Empress Elizabeth had not been such a beauty, the people would not have loved her so much.

1. Prince Charles, marry Camilla Parker Bowles → Lady Diana, not die in a car crash in Paris

2. The Austrian Prince Ferdinand, not be shot in Sarajevo in 1914 → World War I, not break out

3. Napoleon, win the Battle of Waterloo → he, not go into exile to the island of St. Helena

4. The Berlin Wall, not fall in 1989 → the German Democratic Republic and the German Federal Republic, not be reunited

5. General Franco, not die in 1975 → King Carlos, not become King of Spain

6. Austria, not become a member of the European Union in 1995 → we, have a different currency instead of the EURO today

7. Sir Alexander Fleming, not found Penicillin → millions of people, die from infections all over the world in the last decades

8. King George VI., not die at the age of 56 → his daughter Queen Elizabeth II., not celebrate her Diamond Jubilee in 2012

Now add some further sentences yourself.

9.

10.

11.

12.

Two birds were sitting on a tree not far from an airport.
Suddenly a jet plane roared through the sky close by them.
"Gosh, look at that!" said one.
"I bet you would go fast too if your tail was on fire," said the other.

Ziele erreicht? – Super-Challenge: Mixed Types

Finish the sentences below. Mind the correct tenses!

1. If we don't reduce our carbon footprint, the climate on our planet _____
   _____ .

2. If it did not rain so much in Scotland, more tourists _____
   _____ .

3. Countries like the Netherlands or Denmark will be flooded if sea levels _____
   _____ .

4. If Marco Polo had not found a passage to China about 700 years ago, we _____
   _____ .

5. Mozart would not be famous today if _____
   _____ .

6. If tobacco had been banned earlier, fewer people _____
   _____ .

7. People would stay in their jobs longer if _____
   _____ .

8. If housework were shared equally between partners, more women _____
   _____ .

9. If fast food restaurants sold healthier food, fewer children _____
   _____ .

10. Teachers would not suffer burnout so easily if _____
    _____ .

11. If the European Union does not make better laws to monitor banks, _____
    _____ .

12. If the gun laws were tightened in the United States, _____
    _____ .

Self-Check

✓ started ✓✓ on my way ✓✓✓ accomplished	✓	✓✓	✓✓✓
I can distinguish between the four types of conditional clauses.			
I can make appropriate *if*-sentences by using the correct verb forms.			
I can use the different types of conditional clauses in context.			

Indefinite Pronouns and Quantifiers

Die unbestimmten Für- und Zahlwörter

 Meine Ziele

Nach Bearbeitung dieses Kapitels kann ich

- die verschiedenen unbestimmten Zahlwörter unterscheiden und entsprechend verwenden;
- die Quantitätsbezeichnungen im Gebrauch voneinander unterscheiden und richtig anwenden;
- alle unbestimmten Zahlwörter im Kontext korrekt gebrauchen.

 **Task 1: Indefinite Pronouns – *Some* or *Any* and Compounds**

Fill in the correct forms.

1. Jill wanted to buy _____ soy milk, but there was not _____ at the supermarket.

   Instead, she bought _____ low-fat dairy products.

2. At the presentation for the new advertising campaign there was hardly _____ Mr Miller knew.

3. "No, you cannot have _____ more raspberries because I need _____ to make jam."

4. "If you have got _____ further questions, please do not hesitate to ask."

5. "The water is boiling. Do you want _____ tea?" – "Yes, please."

6. "Do you know how to play 'Ludo'?" – "Yes, of course, _____ could tell you. In German it's 'Mensch-Ärgere-Dich-Nicht'."

7. "Excuse me, which bus goes to Linz?" – "You can take _____ bus. They all go to Linz."

8. There was a bowl and _____ cornflakes on the table, but there was not _____ milk

   _____. So Tim stood up, went into the kitchen and got _____.

9. Last Saturday there was a BBQ at the Millers'. Unfortunately, there were not _____ burgers left when

   Tom arrived.

10. "I haven't got _____ stamps, but I need _____ urgently because I have to post the

    letter before noon. Do you have _____?" – "Yes, there are _____ in the drawer."

11. At the conference Mr Smith met _____ interesting people.

12. "I don't care what we will do today. We can do _____ you like."

13. "Come on! Come with us! We won't have _____ fun without you!"

14. If you have _____ problems, ask your teacher.

15. "Oh, no! _____ has spilt _____ milk on the floor." – "Well, it wasn't me. It must

    have been _____ else!"

16. The police officer asked if _____ had seen what had happened.

17. Peter has not had _____ to eat since breakfast.

18. This is a very simple puzzle. _____ can solve it.

19. "We haven't got _____ bread." – "You'd better go to the supermarket because we need

_____ butter and _____ cheese, too." – "_____ else? Would you

like to have _____ cold meat as well?" – "Oh, yes, please."

20. _____ seats in the first few rows are taken, but these seats are not. So you can take

_____ seat you like.

21. "_____ of the students never hand in _____ essays. They are quite lazy", the

professor said angrily.

22. When father came home from work, he did not want _____ to eat because he had been at a business

lunch with _____ of the company's new clients.

23. "Does _____ mind if I open a window?"

24. "Let me know if you need _____, Peter!"

25. "Which song shall I sing?" – "_____. You can sing them all perfectly well."

26. Although the students had studied a lot, hardly _____ of them passed the Spanish grammar test.

27. Mother was too surprised to say _____ .

28. "What is wrong? Have you got _____ in your shoe?"

29. While they were on holidays, _____ broke into their house. _____ rather valuable

rings and necklaces were stolen. Up to now the police have not arrested _____ .

30. Since the invention of the Blackberry, smartphones and other innovative gadgets have made internet access possible

_____ (überall) _____ time.

31. The radio is a background medium because most listeners do _____ else while listening.

32. Nuclear energy is an emission-free source because it does not burn _____ to produce energy.

33. In a Montessori school the children start work by choosing _____ piece of equipment from the

shelves in the classroom.

34. What is market research? It is _____ organised effort to gather information about markets or

customers. But what is a market? Businesses sell to customers in markets. A market is _____ place

where buyers and sellers meet to trade products. _____ business in a marketplace is likely to be in

competition with other firms offering similar products.

35. The term 'acid rain' means _____ form of precipitation that contains harmful substances.

36. Although many adopted children feel positive about their adoption, _____ may question their identity.

37. Underwater Hockey is becoming increasingly popular around the world, and _____ countries have

formed national teams, which take part in world championships.

38. When most people think of the word 'disability' they immediately picture _____ in a wheelchair, but

there are many different types of disability.

39. School violence is _____ form of violent activity inside the school building.

40. Experts have recently come to realise that people can also develop addictions to activities, such as gambling or surfing the internet, going shopping or having sex. What these activities have in common is the person doing them finds them enjoyable in _____ way.

Dad: "Did you have any problems with the exam questions?"
Son: "No, it was the answers I got stuck on."

Task 2: Indefinite Pronouns – *All, Each* or *Every* and Compounds

Fill in the correct forms.

1. _____ family in our road has got a big garden and a swimming pool.

2. _____ day Alice goes to work by bus.

3. The students have got English on _____ of these days: Monday, Tuesday and Friday.

4. _____ cat loves mice, but nearly _____ cats hate dogs.

5. Last year _____ of my students got good marks in _____ subject. _____ got an A* in English.

6. _____ applauded after the presentation of their new advertising campaign.

7. Jason told Betty the truth; he told her _____.

8. My family and I went to the Ars Electronica Center _____ other weekend.

9. As it was cold and rainy _____ day long they stayed at home.

10. Ben meets his uncle and aunt _____ now and then.

11. Britain is one of the most regulated countries in the world when it comes to owning guns. _____ firearm must be registered on a firearm certificate.

12. Nearly _____ day you hear about people being kidnapped, family members getting violent, children being abused, brutal murders and school shootings that have taken place _____ over the world.

13. Violence at school comes in many different forms – and bullying is one form. It is a problem that can affect _____ children.

14. The earth's seven billion humans share many similarities and differences. _____ on earth must eat, breath, and drink to stay alive. _____ has a family, a language, and a culture. _____ people have hopes, dreams, fears, and feelings. And humans differ in many ways, too.

15. Volcano boarding is considered as the coolest sport around the world by many thrill-seeking sports fanatics. Thousands of them head to the foothills of Nicaragua's Cerro Negro Mountain _____ year to take part in this new sporting craze.

16. The Olympic Games are currently held _____ other year, with summer and winter games alternating.

17. The internet has brought the globe into a single room; _____ is at our fingertips. The internet has tremendous potential and a lot to offer in terms of services. However, like _____ single innovation in science and technology the internet has its advantages and disadvantages.

18. The internet has opened up new ways of communication: emails enable people to communicate within seconds. This allows businesses to communicate with their suppliers and consumers located _____ over the world.

19. Young people often put too much of their personal information online for _____ to see and get hold of.

20. With more women in the boardroom, greater equality in legislative rights, and an increasing number of female role models in _____ aspect of life, many of the younger generation feel that _____ battles have been won for women.

21. A tropical rainforest is a complex and fragile ecosystem. _____ is so interdependent that upsetting one part can lead to unknown damage or even destruction of the whole.

22. Marketing has a great influence on almost _____ part of a company's activities.

23. The seven Ps of marketing are a set of tools used to gain an advantage in the marketplace. No element of the marketing mix is more important than another – _____ element ideally supports the others. Companies modify _____ element in the marketing mix to establish an overall brand image and a USP.

24. Due to the global warming sea levels will rise. If _____ glaciers melted today, the seas would rise about 70 metres.

25. In most countries, the state is responsible for the organisation and the content of its education systems so that the schooling and training of _____ students is provided.

26. In a Montessori school the children are _____ in class together, despite their different ages.

27. Nuclear power plants require significantly less land for its construction and operation than _____ other energy sources.

28. Nuclear power stations are not atomic bombs waiting to go off, and they are not prone to 'meltdowns'. If western standards are applied, there is practically no risk at _____ . Multiple safety systems and construction protect the reactor from _____ potential accident.

29. From an early age we are waiting for someone who fits what love researchers refer to as our 'love maps'. _____ love map is unique because _____ has a different idea of what is attractive.

30. Getting married is a once-in-lifetime decision for many people. When people wish to get married, _____ of them expect to stay together 'til death do us part'.

Teacher: "Maggie, you must not use 'a' before a plural –
          you say 'a horse', but not 'a horses'."
Maggie: "But, Miss, in church the vicar always says 'a-men'."

Task 3: Quantifiers – *Much/Many* or *A Lot of* and *Little* or *Few*

Fill in the missing forms by translating the German words given in brackets.

1. There are _____ (viele) books on my desk as I have been studying for my final exam since last Friday.

2. As _____ (viele) people hunt wild animals for sport, _____ (viel) damage has been caused by this kind of hunting.

3. Only _____ (wenige) teenagers do not have a Facebook account today.

4. There is only _____ (wenig) water left in the bottle.

5. "How _____ (viel) did you pay for the tickets?" – Well, they were 34 Euros each."

6. _____ (wenige) people think that there are planets with human life in our universe.

7. Statistics show that being married is getting _____ (weniger) important to couples. Instead, _____ (viele) prefer co-habiting.

8. There are _____ (wenige) areas of the world's oceans that are not affected by pollution.

9. Tigers have been in danger of extinction for _____ (viele) years. Unfortunately, there is _____ (wenig) hope that they will survive, as _____ (viel) their natural habitat has already been destroyed.

10. Luckily, there was _____ (viel) rain last month.

11. "How _____ (viele) people were at the festival last weekend?" – "Well, there were _____ (viele)."

12. My sister Sue has got _____ (viele) acquaintances but only _____ (einige wenige) very good friends.

13. Betty usually spends _____ (viel) time in the shopping mall on Saturdays.

14. As Tom does not care _____ (viel) about a healthy nutrition, he has put on _____ (viel) weight.

15. The exhibition is very popular; _____ (viele) people have visited it so far.

16. Father does not have _____ (viel) time these days because he has got _____ (viel) work to do.

17. Experts believe that there will not be _____ (weniger) CO_2 produced by the industry within the next _____ (paar) years.

18. Only _____ (wenige) teenagers know what they want to do in their future lives.

19. As Tim already suffers from smoker's cough I wish that he would not smoke so _____ (viel). I hope he will quit smoking within the next _____ (paar) weeks.

20. _____ (viel) of the focus in a Montessori lesson is on the sensory perception.

21. _____ (viele) of today's products are becoming 'smart'. Devices such as fridges, microwaves, and dishwashers will have smart technology. The internet refrigerator, for example, uses the technology to make _____ (viele) tasks _____ (viel) easier.

22. _____ (viele) people fear that we will lose control of the new genetically modified organisms.

23. These days _____ (viele) people want to visit the same places, and certain tourist attractions are

becoming _____ (weniger) attractive because of the sheer volume of tourists. These 'honeypot

locations' attract _____ (viel mehr) tourists than the local infrastructure can cater for.

24. Disability discrimination occurs when people with a disability are treated _____ (weniger) fairly than

people without a disability. When most people think of the word 'disability' they immediately picture someone in a

wheelchair, but there are _____ (viele) different types of disability.

25. Getting married is a once-in-lifetime decision for _____ (viele) people. When people wish to get married,

all of them expect to stay together 'till death do us part'.

26. As homosexual couples are increasingly accepted, _____ (viele) are choosing to become parents

through adoption, surrogacy or as foster parents. Although these families face all the challenges that traditional

families encounter, they also have a _____ (einige) unique issues.

27. Reaching puberty and becoming an adult does not only mean fighting parents, but also dealing with

_____ (viele) different issues that may cause problems.

28. Volcano boarding is considered as the coolest sport around the world by _____ (viele) thrill-seeking

sports fanatics. Thousands of them head to the foothills of Nicaragua's Cerro Negro Mountain every year to take part

in this new sporting craze.

29. In social networks there are _____ (viele) people that try to scam for money to trick people into

providing them with bank account information.

30. Nuclear power plants require significantly _____ (weniger) land for its construction and operation than

every other energy sources.

 Ziele erreicht? – Challenge: Quantifiers, Indefinite Pronouns and their Compounds

Fill in the missing forms by translating the German words given in brackets.

Outdoor gyms getting more popular

Kids heading down the slide headfirst while others are balancing on brightly-coloured swings, babies talking gobbledygook in the sandpit, and a golden retriever jumping past with a stick in its mouth – such images bring to mind classic park scenes. But _____ (etwas) else is popping up in the UK's public spaces alongside children's play areas – exercise bikes, high bars and cross trainers for adults. So what is behind this trend? Outdoor gyms – or adult playgrounds – have been growing in popularity in recent years. The Great Outdoor Gym Company (GOGC) was _____ (eine)

of the earliest companies to specialise in providing the equipment in the UK. Launching in 2007, they drew inspiration from the Chinese government which was installing outdoor gym equipment in parks. "Cost and accessibility are the two main barriers for people wanting to exercise," says Charlotte Tarrant of GOGC. "Adult playgrounds remove these barriers, and that's why their popularity has grown." People don't like being told what to do and so often don't respond well to advice even if it is well-intended. The Department of Health recommends adults participate in 150 minutes of physical activity _____ (jede) week and yet _____ (viele) Britons do not achieve this on a weekly basis. The London borough of Camden has nine outdoor gyms – the most of _____ (jede) local authority area in the UK. The council cites research suggesting that 26 % of those who were using the outdoor gyms had never exercised before.

If a council focuses all of its exercise promotion strategy on leisure centres it faces obstacles – there are not _____ (viele) centres, and _____ (einige) people can find them rather frightening places. The idea of an outdoor gym is to place it in people's way. They are often installed next to kids' playgrounds, thus encouraging parents to use _____ (eines) of the fitness equipment while their children play. Even for those without children, putting them in the way by placing them in parks and other open spaces that people cut across on the way to the shops or work has the potential to create regular users.

Elderly users are particularly targeted by _____ (einige) of the adult playgrounds, but most have users of all ages. Margot Bloom, 42, found herself using her local adult playground in Southampton. "I am able to do resistance training as a part of my dog-walking routine. Runners stop to use it and even _____ (einige) serious body builders make use of it to top off their workout. In the summer, the adult playground becomes a bit of a social event with _____ (jede/r) helping _____ (einander) other. I'm not fond of indoor gyms – or their prices."

Andy Sturtevant, 33, who has been using the adult playground in north-west London once or twice a week for the past year, had to give up his gym subscription and soon found outdoor gyms were in _____ (jeder) case more enjoyable. "Adult playgrounds are _____ (viel) better – fresh air, no televisions blaring and a better mix of people. You're more likely to meet Maureen from Meals on Wheels, as I have, at the outside gym than Steve on steroids in the gym. It's always busy when I go and has definitely got busier."

Talking of trends, what's next for the adult playground? The latest product to launch is the green energy gym: People create _____ (viel) electricity by working out so as they pedal away on the bike, they can see the amount of energy they are creating. It is used to light up the fitness zone at night and can even power local buildings. The first of these 'eco wellness' zones in the UK opened in Shaw Park, Hull, last week.

BBC ONLINE – ADAPTED

obstacle = das Hindernis

Self-Check

✓ started   ✓✓ on my way   ✓✓✓ accomplished

	✓	✓✓	✓✓✓
I can use the indefinite pronouns and their compounds correctly in sentences.			
I can differentiate between the various quantifiers and use them appropriately.			
I can use all indefinite pronouns and quantifiers in context.			

Customer: "How much is this melon?"
Greengrocer: "90 p."
Customer: "That's very expensive."
Greengrocer: "You can have half the melon for 50 p."
Customer: "OK, I'll take the other half for 40 p."

Infinitive and Gerund

Infinitiv und Gerundium

 Meine Ziele

Nach Bearbeitung dieses Kapitels kann ich

- in der Verwendung zwischen dem Infinitiv mit und ohne *to* unterscheiden;
- das Gerund richtig bilden und gebrauchen;
- Infinitiv und Gerund im Kontext entsprechend anwenden.

 **Task 1: Infinitive with or without *to***

Fill in *to* where necessary.

1. Ben cannot afford _____ buy anything because he is broke.

2. If you want _____ eat at Fabio's in Vienna, you need _____ book.

3. The professor made his students _____ do the experiment again.

4. My dad promised _____ buy me the festival tickets if I passed my maths test.

5. When I was a teenager my parents hardly ever let me _____ do what I wanted.

6. They did not expect _____ see Tim at the party.

7. "What would you like _____ do tonight?" – "Well, let's _____ go to the cinema."

8. If I were you, I would rather _____ tell him the truth.

9. Luckily, he need not _____ do the test again.

10. My brother wants me _____ fix his mountain bike.

11. It stopped raining. Let's _____ go for a walk

12. The police watched them _____ deal with drugs.

13. There was nothing else _____ do but _____ wait.

14. As Alan has fallen in love with Betty he hopes _____ see her again soon.

15. The doctor warned Mr Miller not _____ work so hard.

16. Mother noticed us _____ come home late.

17. Last Saturday I invited all my friends _____ come to a summer party.

18. Mr Miller saw the burglar _____ break into the neighbour's house.

19. I was really surprised _____ see Sue at the party.

20. "Ben, let your little sister _____ play with her doll!"

21. "What makes Ann _____ think that Tim is betraying her?" – "Well, I do not know."

22. The teacher had his students _____ write the report again.

23. As usual Granny could not decide what _____ have for dessert.

24. I heard my parents _____ quarrel yesterday evening.

25. "Alan, please, help me _____ carry the shopping bags to the kitchen."

26. Sue sadly went away as she saw them _____ whisper.

27. After the baby had just fallen asleep mother asked us not _____ make any noise.

28. As it was already getting dark the guide advised them _____ stay close together.

29. The teacher did not allow his students _____ leave earlier.

30. The police asked Mr Meyers if he had seen the suspect _____ leave the house that morning.

31. "If you do not want to be late you had better _____ go now."

32. As Ben had been so lazy lately, his mother did not permit him _____ go to the concert last Friday.

33. Alice recommended me _____ take custard tart for dessert.

34. "Did you remember _____ return the book?" – "Yes, of course. I already brought it back on Monday."

35. When Jason was in his twenties he used _____ do extreme sports.

36. Tim will _____ help his father in garden tomorrow afternoon.

37. Mother was really upset because Ben did not know how _____ behave.

38. Mr Meyers expects his son _____ become a doctor.

39. The most important question is what they should _____ do next.

40. Mother had Jill _____ share the sweets with her younger siblings.

"I don't want to hear you use those bad words any more."
"But, Mum, Shakespeare uses them all the time."
"Well, don't play with him again."

Task 2: Gerund or Infinitive with or without *to*

Put the verbs in brackets in the correct forms.

1. Jason finally stopped _____ (feel) sick on Monday morning.

2. As Tim has fallen in love with Sue he is looking forward to _____ (see) her again soon.

3. As Nick had not passed his Spanish test, his parents did not permit him _____ (go) to the summer party with his friends.

4. Father will _____ (help) Jason _____ (fix) his bike.

5. Alan cannot stand _____ (hear) his parents quarrel every day.

6. The teacher had his students _____ (share) the books.

7. As it was a sunny and warm day the children were not allowed _____ (play) computer games.

8. The Millers finished _____ (renovate) their house last month.

9. As it was raining heavily, father suggested _____ (go) to the museum.

10. The teacher insisted on _____ (correct) the students' texts.

11. In his youth Bill used _____ (read) a lot of fantasy books.

12. Mr Meyers tried _____ (convince) Tim and Ben _____ (take part) in the sports competition.

13. The manager succeeded in _____ (solve) this difficult problem.

14. Ben apologised to his mother for _____ (have) come home so late.

15. The students were made _____ (write) the report again.

16. The latest book of Dan Brown is really worth _____ (read).

17. Nowadays a lot of people are giving up _____ (smoke).

18. The man denied _____ (have) broken into the Miller's house.

19. The professor made his students _____ (write) the report again.

20. I do not know why, but many students think that they are not good at _____ (write) essays and reports.

21. Tom had better _____ (call) his mother right away.

22. Mr Smith apologised for not _____ (have) called our office earlier.

23. Imagine _____ (go) to the festival next weekend! Wouldn't that be great?

24. After the party mother expected us _____ (clean) up all the rooms.

25. Granny often dreamed of _____ (spend) her holidays in Italy.

26. The man was suspected of _____ (have) caused an accident.

27. The teacher wanted his students _____ (concentrate) on _____ (do) the experiment.

28. We heard the neighbour's children _____ (play) loudly in the garden.

29. Unfortunately, Tom did not care about _____ (be) reminded again and again of his unpunctuality.

30. The teacher made his students _____ (read) all the books on the list.

31. The Millers thanked their friends for _____ (be) so helpful.

32. Father prevented his son from _____ (make) the same mistake again.

33. Mr Meyers, my boss, does not like his employees _____ (be) late.

34. The young man denied _____ (have) sold drugs, but he admitted _____ (know) the dealers.

35. As Betty has a terrible headache she does not feel like _____ (go) out tonight.

36. After having taken him to hospital there was nothing else _____ (do) but _____ (wait) patiently.

37. As it had stopped _____ (rain) father suggested _____ (go) for a walk.

38. Ann would sooner _____ (go) out with her friends than _____ (study) for her maths test.

39. Sue promised not _____ (tell) any lies anymore.

40. When I called Alice she was busy _____ (clean) the bathroom.

 Ziele erreicht? – Challenge 1: Infinitive or Gerund

Fill in the correct forms of the verbs in brackets.

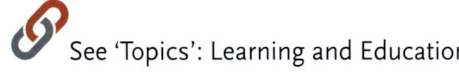 See 'Topics': Learning and Education

The values of a university degree

_____ (go) to university is no small investment in time and money. Given the recent high levels of unemployment worldwide, students _____ (leave) high school may think _____ (go) directly to work makes more financial sense than _____ (go) to college. Yet the global financial crisis has widened the employment and earnings gap between college-educated workers and those with only a secondary education. People with less education have found themselves more likely _____ (be) unemployed and have more difficulty _____ (find) a job, a review of unemployment data from countries around the globe shows.

The value of a university degree, at least when it comes to _____ (find) a job, is not unique to the US. The correlation can also be seen around the world, said Daniel Hamermesh, an international labour economist at the University of Texas in Austin. People with less education have found themselves more likely _____ (be) unemployed.

However, there are exceptions to the overall utility of a college degree when it comes to joblessness, particularly in countries where educational systems are remarkably strong, or where economies are booming. In Japan, for instance, where high school is expected _____ (prepare) some students for a career, the added value of a university education may _____ (be) more limited, with government initiatives also _____ (help) to keep unemployment across the country artificially low. And in an economy like Germany's, managers are hungry _____ (hire) any workers, regardless of their education level.

For most places in the developed world, however, the reality remains: a college degree is practically the new minimum requirement for even the lowest-level jobs at many companies. There is also evidence that _____ (have) the degree is likely to pay off down the road for younger graduates, _____ (offer) hope to jobless young graduates across Europe. OECD research found, for instance, that in Brazil, _____ (have) a tertiary education offered workers a 200 % premium in lifetime earnings compared to those who hadn't finished high school. In Greece, Korea, and Turkey, the premium gap was 70 %. That premium will likely only go up as the economy improves.

"A college degree is always going to lend an advantage," Hamermesh said.

BBC Online – Adapted

Ziele erreicht? – Challenge 2: Infinitive or Gerund

Fill in the correct forms of the verbs in brackets.

 See 'Topics': Food and Health

Children's lunchboxes contain more junk food

Some children are coming to school with cold chips or just a packet of biscuits in their lunchbox, experts say. An online survey of 250 school, youth and health staff _____ (work) with children in England suggests many _____ (go) without enough _____ (eat) during the school day.

The Children's Food Trust's poll found 68.1 % had seen a rise in the proportion of families _____ (struggle) to feed their children in the past two years. Lunchboxes now contain less fruit and more junk food, it suggests.

Of the staff _____ (work) in schools, 47.5 % said they had seen a change in the food in children's lunchboxes as household budgets got tighter. One staff member said they had seen "poorer quality sandwich fillings, sometimes just margarine". He added: "In some ways it is healthier, but some families only give cold cooked rice or cold chips with fish fingers or similar." There were also references to more junk food, sweets and chocolate appearing in lunchboxes, and less fruit. The snapshot survey also found 84.6 % of the professionals who chose _____ (take) part in the survey had seen children without enough _____ (eat) during the course of their work.

Of those who said this, 84.8 % said it applied to about a third of the children they worked with. Children's Food Trust chief executive-designate Linda Cregan said too many people who worked with children were having _____ (go) above and beyond the call of duty to try _____ (protect) children from the effects of hunger and poor diet.

She added: "Of course it's a parent's responsibility _____ (make) sure their child eats well. But as this and other surveys have shown, the reality is that this can _____ (be) an enormous struggle. Whether we like it or not, people _____ (work) in these jobs are at the front line of _____ (help) parents on this, so they need the right support. As local authorities develop their public health plans, ring-fencing funding _____ (support) children's nutrition would be a good starting point. This could be used in all sorts of ways – _____ (train) on cooking skills for local organisations _____ (work) with families, _____ (subsidise) good school food, breakfast clubs in schools or grub clubs for the holidays – but _____ (make) that absolute commitment is vital."

Pupils at Priory School in Lewes told the BBC's School Report project their lunches were generally quite good. "I haven't seen people with chips in their lunchboxes – but the school does _____ (offer) chips on Fridays though. I guess people just get that," said Flora, aged 14. Ellen, aged 13, agreed that most people were quite healthy: "I take a piece of fruit to school every day."

School dinners were easier, quicker and nicer because "you can get hot food", according to Ossia, 14. And 13-year-old Safi said: "Packed lunches are cheaper. I can _____ (buy) in bulk and have the same thing every day."

BBC ONLINE – ADAPTED

to subsidise = subventionieren
grub (Singular, umgangssprachlich) = Essen, ‚Fressalien'

Self-Check

✓ started ✓✓ on my way ✓✓✓ accomplished	✓	✓✓	✓✓✓
I can use the infinitive with and without to correctly.			
I can distinguish between the usage of gerund and infinitive forms in sentences.			
I can use infinitive and gerund forms appropriately in context.			

Woman: "Doctor, I have been worried about my husband for months. He keeps thinking he is a chicken."
Doctor: "Good God, why didn't you come and see me earlier?"
Woman: "I would have, but we needed the eggs."

Modal Auxiliary Verbs

Die modalen Hilfsverben

 **Meine Ziele**

Nach Bearbeitung dieses Kapitels kann ich

■ die verschiedenen Formen der Hilfsverben in allen Zeiten richtig bilden;

■ die Umschreibungsformen im Kontext adäquat anwenden.

 **Task: Modal Auxiliary Verbs**

Fill in the correct form of the verb in brackets.

1. Jason is a very sporty person. Unfortunately, he broke his leg last week. So he _____ (nicht können) do any sport for seven days now.

2. In cities dogs _____ (müssen) be kept on a lead. Otherwise you _____ (müssen) pay a fine.

3. You _____ (nicht brauchen) phone her, because she is not in her office at the moment.

4. Figures show that the number of obese children is constantly rising. Consequently, they _____ (eigentlich nicht sollen) eat much food high in calories and sweets. Instead, they _____ (sollen) eat more fruit and vegetables.

5. As Tom is ill he _____ (nicht können) help us tomorrow. That is why we _____ (müssen) do the presentation on the new advertising campaign without him.

6. There are often arguments between parents and their teenage children because lots of parents think their children _____ (müssen) do as they say.

7. "Peter _____ (nicht müssen) be at home by eight. So, why _____ (ich, müssen) be at home by six?"

8. Although Elizabeth is only five years old, she _____ (können) read well.

9. "I observed a robbery yesterday. What _____ (soll) I do?" – "You _____ (eigentlich sollen) report it to the police."

10. People _____ (nicht dürfen) smoke on buses.

11. The Meyers have two houses, three cars and a yacht. I think they _____ (müssen) earn a lot of money.

12. Sue _____ (nicht brauchen) go shopping yesterday because there was still enough food at home.

13. We _____ (müssen) go now because the last bus will leave in 10 minutes.

14. Last week he got a bad mark in his German test. That is why he _____ (nicht dürfen) go to Jim's birthday party on Saturday.

15. Mother _____ (nicht brauchen) clean the flat because her children had already done it for her.

16. Mobile phones _____ (müssen) be switched off during the flight.

17. "The roads are icy. You _____ (sollen) drive more slowly."

18. "You have got a temperature. You _____ (eigentlich sollen) see a doctor as soon as possible."

19. The student _____ (nicht brauchen) ask his teacher because he had already found the explanation in the book.

20. Mother fears that Jason _____ (müssen) do the test again.

21. When we were at school we _____ (müssen) wear school uniforms.

22. On the safari we _____ (können vielleicht) see elephants.

23. Members of the diplomatic service _____ (nicht brauchen) open their suitcases at the customs.

24. Granny _____ (müssen) do all the work by herself since her husband died two years ago.

25. "Look at those black clouds! It _____ (könnte) start raining."

26. The children _____ (nicht dürfen) play there.

27. Tim _____ (nicht können) swim until he was ten.

28. "Jason _____ (nicht brauchen) send me these flowers, but I am glad that he did!"

29. Luckily, the Millers _____ (können) sell their old flat before they bought a new one; so they _____ (nicht brauchen) borrow any money from the bank.

30. Since the invention of smartphones and other innovative gadgets internet addiction has become a serious health problem for many so that leading psychiatrists say it _____ (sollen) be officially recognised as a clinical disorder.

31. Watching too much TV _____ (könnte) trigger violence and aggression, especially in children and teenagers.

32. If research is to be believed, we _____ (könnten) sit on a time bomb. Recently conducted studies have found out that the regular use of a mobile phone _____ (können) pose various health risks. As children are particularly at risk they _____ (nicht sollen) use mobile phones unless it is absolutely necessary.

33. As the media works with subtle mechanisms, we often do not realise that we are influenced by it. So we _____ (sollen) be aware of the manipulative power of the media.

34. Trading globally gives consumers and countries the opportunity to purchase goods and service not available in their own countries. Almost every kind of product _____ (können) be found on the international market.

35. At the beginning of the 20th century school discipline was quite strict: pupils _____ (müssen) listen to their teachers and follow their instructions. Teachers treated their pupils like children who _____ (dürfen) speak only when they were spoken to.

36. The seven Ps of marketing are a set of tools used to gain an advantage in the marketplace. A business _____ (nicht können) force a customer to spend money, but they _____ (können) use the Ps to help maximise the product's potential.

37. Advertisers _____ (müssen) have effective media plans in order to reach the maximum number of people. They _____ (sollen) know about the appropriate advertising medium and the target group.

38. In most European countries, the law defines that, in a marriage, both husband and wife _____ (müssen) do equal shares of the household chores and are both responsible for the children's upbringing.

39. Child labour _____ (können) be found in nearly every industry. Most child labourers _____ (müssen) work under conditions that are considered illegal, dangerous or extremely exploitative.

40. The Carbon Footprint allows us to calculate the amount of human pressure on our planet. If our Carbon Footprint indicates that we use more natural resources than the earth supplies, we _____ (müssen) ask ourselves how we _____ (können) reduce our Carbon Footprint so that future generations _____ (können) enjoy the world as we are doing today.

 Ziele erreicht? – Challenge: Modal Auxiliary Verbs

First, read the following text carefully.

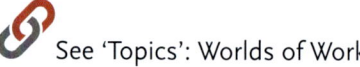 See 'Topics': Worlds of Work

How to survive an office party I

Here are a few tips on how to survive your company's summer gathering:

■ **Graciously attend.** "Even if you dread such events, it is important to show up. Management is throwing the party to thank employees, and to miss it is bad form," said Sue Fox, author of the book Business Etiquette for Dummies. "You don't want to be known for never attending."

■ **Don't stand out.** You will be examined rather carefully if you drink too much alcohol, make rude or dirty remarks, behave in a manner that wouldn't fit in your workplace or dress inappropriately – casual-Friday clothes are usually safe, as is a modest swimsuit if there is a call for such an outfit. Don't forget that any faux pas may end up being posted on social media. And, perhaps most importantly, even if you end up drinking a bit too much or saying something you regret, you must show up at work the next day or people will surely be talking.

■ **Prep your guests.** Most companies encourage employees to bring both partners and children to picnics. It is important to discuss appropriate behaviour beforehand.

"Imagine it is your kid that jumps so aggressively in the bouncy castle that it pops," said Cathy Johnson, a Houston, Texas-based caterer with several corporate clients. Worse yet, what if your spouse takes this opportunity to complain about your long hours at the office? Make sure family members know what is off limits.

■ **Mingle.** It is easy to stick with your closest colleagues, but make an effort to expand your office network, including getting to know the higher-ups. Still, Fox warned, "Remember it is a picnic, not a job interview, and not everyone will want to talk shop."

■ **Play ball.** Joining in games or other contests allows you to be viewed as a team player. Play your best, but, Fox noted, play fair and be a good sport. It is okay to admit you don't know the rules or have never played before.

BBC ONLINE – ADAPTED

to talk shop = über die Arbeit reden

Now write a list of ten dos and don'ts at a company outing. Use an auxiliary modal (*can/could, may, must, must not, shall/should*, etc.) verb in each sentence, e.g.:

■ You must not miss the party because you are expected to show up.
■ Everybody should attend even if they don't like picnics.
■ Nobody can stay at home because the boss might be offended.

1. _____
2. _____
3. _____
4. _____
5. _____
6. _____
7. _____
8. _____
9. _____
10. _____

Self-Check

✓ started ✓✓ on my way ✓✓✓ accomplished	✓	✓✓	✓✓✓
I can build the different expressions for modal auxiliary verbs in all tenses and use them in sentences correctly.			
I can use all auxiliary modal verbs appropriately in context.			

Nouns and Articles

Das Hauptwort und seine Artikel

🎯 **Meine Ziele**

Nach Bearbeitung dieses Kapitels kann ich

- bestimmte und unbestimmte Artikel korrekt setzen;
- Hauptwörter und ihre Artikel im Kontext adäquat verwenden.

 **Task 1: The Indefinite Article**

Fill in *a* or *an* where necessary.

1. I think we should buy _____ new car. We have had this one for ages.

2. We were having _____ lovely picnic until my wife was stung by _____ bee.

3. "Do not phone at seven this evening. We will be having _____ dinner then."

4. Last year they went to France and skied on _____ Mount Blanc.

5. Ann bought _____ pair of jeans last week.

6. Ben and Jill met at _____ speed-dating event.

7. "What _____ fantastic idea!"

8. This was such _____ difficult test. Hardly any of the students passed it.

9. Sue asked for _____ cup of tea, but she got _____ coffee instead.

10. Alice does not really like _____ sweet things, but she loves _____ chocolate.

11. Yesterday Nick did not have _____ time for breakfast. As his alarm clock had stopped, he was in _____ hurry to get to the meeting in _____ time.

12. As Betty always gets _____ good marks, she must be _____ very intelligent girl.

13. Crocodiles are _____ reptiles.

14. Phil and Mary visit Granny twice _____ month.

15. _____ Ferrari can go more than 300 km _____ hour.

16. Donald Trump is _____ president of the United States.

17. "What _____ loud music! There must be _____ party nearby."

18. Ms Meyers can speak _____ French and _____ Spanish fluently.

19. "Do you want _____ orange?" – "No, thank you. I do not like _____ oranges. I prefer _____ apples and bananas."

20. "I have got such _____ headache. Do you have _____ aspirin?"

21. Liz always has _____ cheese sandwich and _____ tea for breakfast.

22. In 2010 Gerlinde Kaltenbrunner climbed _____ Mount Everest.

23. "Is Jason _____ American or _____ Australian?" – "None of the two. He is _____ Englishman."

24. "I can't find my English book. Have you seen it?" – "Well, there is _____ book over there on the desk, but I don't
know whether it is _____ English one or not."

25. Although Tim is already 28, he still lives at _____ home with his parents.

26. Tom normally goes to work by _____ bus or by _____ train.

27. Mum is terrified of _____ spiders.

28. In some British schools the students have to wear _____ uniforms.

29. "Do you want _____ hamburger or _____ cheeseburger?" – "Well, I would like to have _____ hotdog, if possible."

30. "What _____ amazing view over the rolling hills you've got from here!"

Little Penny: "Dad, how do you spell Mississippi?"
Father: "The river or the state?"

Task 2: Definite and Indefinite Articles

Fill in *a, an* or *the* where necessary.

1. Last Friday Tom had _____ accident with his car. He jumped _____ red light and hit _____ police car.

2. "Do you have _____ pet?" – "Yes, I have had _____ dog all my life. At the moment I have _____ dog, two cats and
three hamsters." – "Well, I would like to have _____ dog, but I am not sure about _____ cats and _____ hamsters."

3. Father told his son not to cross _____ street.

4. Peter declaimed Goethe's most famous poem "Der Erlkönig" in _____ loud voice.

5. As two of his colleagues were ill last week, Tim had to work more than ten hours _____ day.

6. Sue has always had _____ passion for _____ Italian food. That's why she goes on _____ holiday to _____ Tuscany
twice _____ year.

7. After having _____ accident Nick was taken to _____ hospital.

8. As Betty is on _____ diet she does not eat _____ sweets.

9. "When I was at _____ school, we had to stand up when _____ teacher came into _____ room.", Granny said.

10. Father did not ask _____ price of Ben's new car, but he knew it had cost _____ fortune.

11. We both work full-time, but my husband never lifts _____ finger. He expects me to do all _____ housework.

12. Ben works hard to keep fit. On _____ Mondays, _____ Wednesdays, and _____ Fridays he gets up at _____ dawn for
training. Even in _____ winter months, when _____ temperature is often freezing, he never misses _____ session.

13. Footballer Cristiano Ronaldo was injured in _____ second half of _____ match in _____ tackle with _____
goalkeeper.

14. Whenever Tom eats _____ shellfish he gets _____ stomach-ache.

15. Jason hates _____ heights. When he looks down he feels dizzy.

16. Ben completely ruined our holiday; he was in _____ bad mood for _____ whole week.

17. With both children at _____ university, _____ house seems really quiet.

18. We head Sue playing _____ piano.

19. Last Friday I noticed _____ girl shoplifting. I saw her take _____ lipstick from shelf and put it in her bag.

20. In _____ summer _____ most people go on _____ holidays to _____ Italy or _____ Spain.

21. Last Friday night Tom gave me _____ lift because I had missed _____ last bus.

22. "Where is _____ nearest post office?" – "Well, just opposite _____ church."

23. _____ customs officer looked carefully at _____ signature.

24. Mr Miller told _____ police that he could not remember _____ accident clearly.

25. This is _____ most interesting project I have ever done!

26. Adam is _____ sporty person. He normally goes to _____ work by _____ bike, but today he is taking _____ bus because it is raining heavily.

27. These days _____ doctors do not understand why _____ number of _____ people who are physically active is constantly decreasing.

28. Rebecca is very good at _____ languages; she can speak three languages fluently.

29. When she was _____ teenager Ann was _____ excellent tennis player. Unfortunately, she broke her ankle _____ year ago. Since then she has not been able to play _____ tennis at _____ high level anymore.

30. Last week Betty was working really hard for her presentation. She hardly took _____ break, but it was worth _____ effort. She did _____ excellent presentation and was able to answer all _____ difficult questions. Betty got _____ incredibly good feedback from _____ examiners. She finally got _____ A*.

What do you get if you cross a tulip with a camel?
A flower that can last for days without water.

Fill in *a*, *an* or *the* where necessary.

 See 'Topics': Worlds of Work

How to survive an office party II

Alex Abrams has always been competitive and ambitious. That's how _____ then first-year associate found herself in front of _____ large bowl of hot dogs and _____ baked beans at her New York law firm's July barbecue. Her boss had asked her to participate in _____ annual hot dog eating contest. "Of course, I had to win," said Abrams, now 33-years old. Abrams closed her eyes, slathered _____ first dog in ketchup, and downed it. She kept going. She was concentrating so hard that she missed _____ signal the contest was over. Eventually Abrams looked up to find her new colleagues watching in awe. She had eaten _____ 21 sausages – three times more than anyone else – in just under 12 minutes. "Eight years later, certain partners still only know me as 'Franks,'" Abrams said.

While there is some evidence that company picnics are _____ growing phenomenon in _____ United Kingdom, they are primarily _____ US tradition. _____ recession brought some cutbacks to such gatherings, but surveys in recent years suggest that _____ office mates will once again find themselves together for company softball games, picnics or corporate beach parties. About 55 % of American companies had _____ company picnic, according to _____ Society of Human Resources survey.

Outside of _____ United States, summer outings are not as common, although spending some free time with managers is widespread in other cultures. In _____ Japan, for instance, socializing with _____ boss at _____ karaoke bar or other nightspots after business hours is often required.

In the US, bosses often see out-of-office summer outings as _____ chance to bond as team, to boost morale and to reward hard work. For _____ employees, however, it's not so simple. While having fun with _____ colleagues and their families, workers must be careful to not have so much fun that those same people are whispering about you at _____ office for months afterward. Many employees dislike _____ tradition, saying they have no interest in socialising with _____ co-workers during precious free time.

_____ other problems can arise when colleagues meet outside their usual environment. To battle social uneasiness, some find themselves drinking too much. Employees lose their ability to rein in their own inappropriate behaviour when drinking at _____ events like company picnics, showed _____ study conducted by _____ University of Birmingham in England.

Still, it's important to remember that office outings can be valuable networking opportunities. _____ best approach going in? Think of them as _____ work. "Your boss will be there, maybe your boss's boss," said Karen Burns, _____ careers blogger based in Seattle. "Which, sadly, makes it not _____ party but _____ business function."

That's _____ lesson Abrams learned _____ hard way. "I'm Jewish, don't eat pork, had never had _____ hot dog before that day," she said. Twenty-one hot dogs later, she fell ill and had to be driven home – by her boss. "He seemed less than impressed," she said.

BBC ONLINE – ADAPTED

to slather (US) = tief in Ketchup tauchen

Ziele erreicht? – Challenge 2: Definite and Indefinite Articles

Fill in *a* or *the* where necessary.

See 'Topics': Addiction and Dependence

Internet addiction influences users' wellbeing

_____ Internet addicts can suffer _____ form of cold turkey when they stop using _____ web – just like people coming off drugs, according to research. _____ study by Swansea and Milan universities found _____ young people had "negative moods" when they stopped surfing _____ net. Heavy internet-users also tended to be more depressed, _____ research found.

The results are part of _____ study looking at _____ negative psychological impacts of the internet. The university said over _____ past decade internet addiction had become widely debated in _____ medical literature. Its research said _____ so-called addicts' web usage was varied, but it was common for them to gamble and access pornography online.

_____ Internet addiction is said to be _____ clinical disorder marked by out-of-control internet use. Prof Phil Reed, of _____ Swansea University's college of human and health sciences, said: "Although we do not know exactly what _____ internet addiction is, our results show that around half of _____ young people we studied spend so much time on _____ net that it has negative consequences for _____ rest of their lives. When these people come off-line, they suffer increased negative mood – just like people coming off illegal drugs like _____ ecstasy.

These initial results, and related studies of brain function, suggest that there are some nasty surprises waiting on _____ net for people's wellbeing. These results confirm _____ previous reports regarding psychological characteristics and traits of internet users, but go beyond those findings to show _____ immediate effect of _____ internet on _____ mood of those who are addicted."

_____ study explored the immediate impact of internet exposure on _____ mood and psychological states of internet addicts and low internet-users. _____ 60 volunteers, made up of 27 men and 33 women aged in their 20s, were given psychological tests to explore _____ levels of addiction, mood, anxiety, depression and autism traits. They were then given exposure to _____ internet for 15 minutes and re-tested for mood and anxiety. _____ research found _____ mood of high internet-users suffered after _____ internet use compared to low internet-users. Scientists said this could possibly trigger them to log back on to _____ internet to "remove these unpleasant feelings".

Research into _____ internet addiction has also been carried out in China. Last year experts there said web addicts had brain changes similar to those hooked on drugs or _____ alcohol. They scanned _____ brains of 17 young web addicts and found disruption in the way their brains were wired up.

BBC ONLINE – ADAPTED

Self-Check

✓ started ✓✓ on my way ✓✓✓ accomplished

	✓	✓✓	✓✓✓
I can choose the correct definite and indefinite articles in sentences.			
I can use nouns and articles appropriately in context.			

The Passive Voice

Das Passiv

Meine Ziele

Nach Bearbeitung dieses Kapitels kann ich
- Sätze aus dem Aktiv ins Passiv transferieren;
- Sätze im Passiv spontan bilden und im Kontext korrekt verwenden.

Task: Passive Voice

Put the following sentences into Passive Voice.

1. Drug mules smuggle drugs in containers or packets from Latin America to Europe.

2. The mass media transmits information to a large audience.

3. The media uses subtle mechanisms in order to influence and manipulate us.

4. TV companies integrate advertisements into their TV shows.

5. The process of global warming threatens humans as well as animals and plants.

6. Watching too much TV can trigger violence and aggression in children and teenagers.

7. GM food might reduce hunger in developing countries.

8. The US Defence Department developed a communication network in the 1960s.

9. Government agencies and universities used the new communication network to share information and data.

10. Most people drink alcohol moderately.

11. Motorola released the first commercially available mobile phone in 1983.

12. People have been sending text messages since 1995.

13. The burning of coal, oil and gas causes global warming.

14. Drug couriers swallow the drugs in capsules in order to evade airport security.

15. Environmental factors drive animals from their natural habitats.

16. Thomas Jefferson wrote the US American Constitution in 1787.

17. Overweight people should do a lot of exercise.

18. We ought to eat five portions of fruit and vegetables every day.

19. Scottish scientists cloned the first mammal – Dolly, the sheep – in 1997.

20. Vertical farms will make fresh products less expensive.

21. GM food can trigger allergies in humans.

22. The IMF and the World Bank have created global financial markets.

23. Technology and the internet have turned the world into a small village.

24. Since more and more companies are outsourcing work to Asian countries, a lot of Europeans are losing their jobs.

25. Fairtrade offers farmers and workers improved terms of trade.

26. Vertical farming can reverse global warming.

27. The Internet of Things will change people's everyday life radically.

28. At the beginning of the 20th century teachers treated their pupils like children.

29. Today teachers treat their pupils in a more respectful way.

30. In the last few years, many businesses have developed a lot of new technologies.

31. British state schools outlawed corporal punishment in 1986.

32. Advertising keeps customers informed about new products.

33. Governments should forbid adverts on children's channels.

34. Every country should provide sufficient schooling and training for all students.

35. The glass ceiling keeps women from getting access to the best jobs in a company.

36. Norway has already introduced female quotas.

37. In a marriage, both husband and wife have to do equal shares of the household chores.

38. People do recreational activities for a number of reasons.

39. Tourism provides jobs in many areas.

40. Two Union Army officers founded the NRA in 1871.

Ziele erreicht? – Challenge: Passive Voice

Fill in the correct forms of the verbs in brackets. Mind the tenses!

 See 'Topics': Addiction and Dependence

Is smoking water-pipes really harmless?

You might call it 'shisha' in Egypt and Sudan, 'nargile' in Turkey and Syria or 'hookah' in India. Maybe you know it simply as hubble-bubble. Some _____ (make) from clay, others from beautifully carved metals or plastics. However, the principle is the same – these water-pipes allow you to smoke flavoured tobacco as it _____ (bubble) through water. They are now gaining in popularity in India and the Middle East, where they _____ (say) to have originated.

This shisha cafe culture has also extended to Europe, Brazil and the United States. Many hookah cafes _____

_____ (open) both in larger cities like London as well as in college towns, and a recent study found that as many as a fifth of American students has tried it. In many countries these pipes _____ (see) as safe enough not to be subject to legislation on smoking in public places. But the idea that these pipes are harmless is a myth.

One of the main misconceptions is that the risks of tobacco _____ (minimise) because it _____ (purify) as it passes through the water. However, this ignores the complete source of the smoke that enters your mouth.

The tobacco _____ (burn) in a small dish on top of the main body of the water-pipe. You inhale through a mouthpiece connected by a pipe to a reservoir of water at the bottom. As you breathe in, smoke _____ _____ (draw) from the burning tobacco and bubbles through the water up into your mouth. The tobacco _____ (sweet) with glycerine, and charcoal _____ (add) to keep the tobacco burning. This means the smoke inhaled contains several toxic substances, including carbon monoxide, heavy metals and tar. Some water-pipes _____ (sell) with mouthpieces containing cotton filters or a plastic net, but a report by the World Health Organisation says there is no evidence that these mouthpieces reduce the harm.

Many people think that smoking shisha is less dangerous than smoking a cigarette. It is true that the smoke _____ (cool) by the water which possibly makes an individual puff less harmful. However, in a typical hour-long session a person can inhale the equivalent of 100 to 200 times the smoke from a single cigarette. In a study in Florida, USA, customers' carbon monoxide levels _____ (test) as they left bars that allowed the smoking either of cigarettes or hookah pipes. The people leaving the bars that had water-pipes had triple the levels of carbon monoxide in their bodies. Some reported feeling high, which experts say could have been the early stages of carbon monoxide poisoning.

And what do we know about any long-term consequences? Here, the science is incomplete, as long-term studies of the kind conducted on cigarette tobacco _____ (not, carry) out yet. Researchers admit there is little evidence but suggest that smokers of water-pipes could be at long-term risk for nicotine dependence, cardiovascular disease and even cancer.

So bear in mind one thing: Whether you call it shisha or hubble-bubble, it might smell nice, but it is not as harmless as you might think.

BBC ONLINE – ADAPTED

clay = der Ton
charcoal = die Holzkohle
tar = der Teer

Self-Check

✓ started   ✓✓ on my way   ✓✓✓ accomplished

	✓	✓✓	✓✓✓
I can transfer sentences into the passive voice.			
I can form correct sentences in the passive voice.			
I can use verbs in the passive voice appropriately in context.			

A man travelling at 130 miles per hour on the motorway was stopped by the traffic police.
"Sorry, officer," said the driver, "was I driving too fast?!"
"No, sir", answered the police officer, "you were flying too low."

Relative Clauses

Die Relativsätze

 **Meine Ziele**

Nach Bearbeitung dieses Kapitels kann ich

- die verschiedenen Relativpronomen richtig verwenden;
- erkennen, wann ich ein Relativpronomen wegfallen lassen kann.

 **Task: Relative Pronouns**

Fill in the correct relative pronouns. Put them in brackets if they can be left out.

1. The best restaurant _____ I know is in Rodeo Drive.

2. One should try to stop smoking, _____ is a very bad habit.

3. _____ he had discovered surprised everyone.

4. "Is this the book _____ you were asking for?"

5. I have said _____ I wanted to say.

6. Tom cannot speak French very well, _____ made it difficult for him to follow the conversation.

7. Meeting George Clooney is the only thing _____ a lot of women dream of.

8. Last Saturday I met Mary _____ asked me to give you that.

9. The girl and the cat _____ we saw in the garden yesterday are terribly afraid of dogs.

10. Tim did not help his parents in the garden, _____ made his father rather angry.

11. You will be punished for _____ you have done.

12. The pilot was the only man _____ survived the crash.

13. She expects me to clean the house in half an hour, _____ is impossible.

14. Jill did _____ she could, _____ was not much.

15. The lady _____ is talking to Mr Smith is a famous actress.

16. This is the man _____ Susan would like to marry.

17. I was the only person _____ saw the difficulty _____ was arising.

18. _____ was the most interesting book _____ you have ever read?

19. _____ mother does not like at all is smoking in the bedroom.

20. Everything _____ Jason told his father was completely true.

21. She said that the men were thieves, _____ turned out to be true.

22. As an au pair Ann had to look after children _____ were terribly spoilt.

23. I gave him all _____ he wanted.

24. The company _____ Tom works for is sending him to a conference in London.

25. A girl _____ name I cannot remember gave me this CD on the party last weekend.

26. Father wanted me to come at half past two, _____ did not suit me.

27. The first pupil _____ finds the correct solution will be the winner.

28. Granny could not remember the boy's name, _____ was rather embarrassing.

29. All _____ could be done was to wait.

30. My parents wanted to buy the house _____ was situated near the river.

31. Eating disorders occur when a person's attitude to food weight and body size leads to strict inflexible eating and exercise habits _____ endanger one's health and personal happiness. Factors _____ contribute a lot to eating disorders are low self-esteem, depression and troubled families or difficult relationships. Treatment of eating disorders is difficult; the most important thing _____ family and friends can do is to love the person.

32. The radio is a universal medium _____ can be enjoyed at home, at work, or while driving.

33. Online advertising is a form of promotion _____ uses the internet to attract customers.

34. One of the most important aims _____ advertisers must have in mind before the start their campaign is the target group.

35. The glass ceiling is an imaginary barrier _____ keeps women from getting access to the best jobs in a company.

36. Social networking is most popular online because the internet is filled with millions of individuals _____ want to meet other people, to gather and share first-hand information or to develop friendships. It is quite popular among teenagers, _____ often do not realise the potential danger _____ comes with social networking online. They are usually naïve, _____ makes them an easy prey for criminals. There are a lot of people _____ try to scam for their money. Furthermore, young users often put too much of their personal information online, _____ might reduce the chances of getting a job. Last but not least, a lot of links _____ are passed around via social networking websites are dangerous to click on.

37. GM foods can potentially produce higher crop yields _____ are seen as a way of feeding the world's growing population.

38. The WTO currently has 164 members, _____ represent more than 90 % of the total world trade, and 23 observers _____ are seeking membership. It is governed by a ministerial conference _____ meets every other year. WTO decisions are absolute, and every member must abide by its rulings. It is the WTO _____ acts as judge and jury. In the last decade the WTO has been criticised by people _____ are worried about the effects of free trade and economic globalisation.

39. Fairtrade is an alternative approach to conventional trade _____ is based on a partnership between producers and consumers and _____ promotes fairer trading. Fairtrade offers farmers and workers improved terms of trade, _____ empowers them to combat poverty and strengthen their position.

40. Innovative methods and new technologies, _____ have been developed over centuries, are offering a

significant improvement over established technology. These developments and innovations _____ are

being developed in various areas can contribute a lot to the improvement of human living conditions.

Ziele erreicht? – Challenge: Relative Pronouns

Fill in the missing pronouns.

See 'Topics': Power to the People

The Role of the Royal Family

Members of the Royal Family support The Queen in her many State and national duties, as well as carrying out important work in the areas of public and charitable service and helping to strengthen national unity and stability.

Those _____ undertake official duties are members of The Queen's close family: her children, grandchildren and their spouses, and The Queen's cousins (the children of King George VI's brothers) and their spouses.

Every year the Royal Family as a whole carries out over 2,000 official engagements throughout the UK and worldwide, _____ may include official State responsibilities as well. Members of the Royal Family often carry out official duties in the UK and abroad where The Queen cannot be present in person.

When official events such as receptions, State banquets and garden parties are held, the Royal Family supports The Queen in making her guests welcome. Members of the Royal Family also often represent The Queen and the nation in Commonwealth or other countries, at events such as State funerals or national festivities, or through longer visits to strengthen Britain's diplomatic and economic relations.

The Royal Family also plays an important role in supporting and encouraging the public and charity sectors. About 3,000 organisations list a member of the Royal Family as patron or president.

The huge range of these organisations – _____ cover every subject from education to the environment, hospitals to housing – allows members of the Royal Family to meet people from a wide spectrum of national and local life, and to understand their interests, problems and concerns.

2,000: the number of official engagements _____ are carried out by the Royal Family each year in the UK and overseas.

70,000: the number of people _____ are entertained each year to dinners, lunches, receptions and garden parties at the Royal residences.

100,000: the number of letters _____ are received and answered each year by the Royal Family.

Some members of the Royal Family have also established their own charities – for example, The Prince's Trust, The Duke of Edinburgh's Award Scheme and The Princess Royal Trust for Carers, _____ is a charity which provides advice and support for people acting as carers.

The Royal Family also plays an important role in recognising and supporting the work of the Armed Services. Members of the Royal Family _____ have official relationships with many units of the Forces, pay regular visits to soldiers, sailors and airmen serving at home and abroad.

Finally, the Royal Family as a whole plays a role in strengthening national unity. Members of the Royal Family are able to recognise and participate in community and local events in every part of the UK, from the opening of new buildings to celebrations or acts of commemoration.

The Queen working by herself would be unable to attend every engagement to _____ she is invited. Members of the Royal Family can undertake local or specialist engagements _____ would otherwise have to be declined.

ROYAL.UK

Self-Check

✓ started   ✓✓ on my way   ✓✓✓ accomplished

	✓	✓✓	✓✓✓
I can choose if the relative pronoun can be left out.			
I can use all relative pronouns appropriately in context.			

A man who went to an animal auction found just what he wanted: a beautiful African parrot which he decided to bid for. The bids went higher and higher. Finally the man managed to get the bird for £ 899, which was the highest price ever paid for a parrot in an auction.

As soon as he had bought the bird, the man suddenly remembered that he had forgotten to find out the most important thing about the parrot.
"Does he talk?" he asked the auctioneer anxiously.

"Well, who do you think was bidding against you all the time?"
was the reply.

The Reported Speech

Die indirekte Rede

Meine Ziele

Nach Bearbeitung dieses Kapitels kann ich

- Sätze von der direkten in die indirekte Rede transferieren;
- die richtige Wortfolge in der indirekten Frage einhalten;
- die Infinitivkonstruktion beim indirekten Befehl korrekt bilden;
- die indirekte Rede in allen Varianten bei Berichten und eigenen Erzählungen anwenden.

Task 1: Reported Speech

Change into reported speech.

1. Mr Smith answered, "You can phone from this office."

2. Tom promised, "I will wait for you at the train station."

3. Jason says, "I want to be a famous actor when I am grown up."

4. Jill explained, "I usually take my dog for a walk after I have come home from work."

5. Mary admitted, "The party last Saturday was very funny."

6. Lucy remarked, "In this village nothing ever happens."

7. Tim said, "I have missed my train. So I will be late for work."

8. The shop assistant replied, "Sales already started last weekend."

9. Father says to John, "Tomorrow we are going to meet Granny."

10. Aunt Macy added, "If you are short of money, I can lend you some."

11. Jason replied, "I have already had something for lunch. So you do not have to prepare anything for me."

12. Father explained to Peter, "You don't have to water the flowers. I already did it for you."

13. Paul added, "I have just bought a new car."

14. The speaker announces, "The workshop will start in 5 minutes."

15. Father said to Tom, "You are not allowed to smoke in the living room. If you want to smoke, you have to go outside."

16. The teacher said to the pupils, "You are always making the same mistakes. You should learn more and study more intensively. Otherwise you will not be able to pass your A-levels."

17. Andrew complained, "I have been waiting for Sue for two hours."

18. Father says, "Tom, you have to hurry up. Otherwise you will miss your train."

19. Mother remarked sadly, "I don't think that he will pass his maths test because he has been quite lazy recently."

20. Peter grumbled, "I hate getting up early in the morning."

21. The teacher explained the pupils, "The river Seine flows through Paris."

22. The policeman said, "There has been an accident, and the road is blocked. It will be clear within half an hour."

23. Carol explained, "Here are the books you asked for yesterday."

24. The professor said to the students, "I have left some books on this table here. I think you will find them very useful."

25. Mother explained, "The pond will probably freeze tonight. So we will possibly be able to skate on it tomorrow."

 ## Task 2: Reported Questions

Form reported questions.

1. Mother wanted to know, "Where have you been, Sue?"

2. Father asked Joe, "Can you post the letter for me, please?"

3. Jill begged, "Mum, can you lend me some money? I am penniless."

4. Pat wants to know, "What are you going to do tomorrow?"

5. Paul asked, "How do you get on with your father-in-law?"

6. Sue wanted to know, "Did you like your last holiday?"

7. Alan asked Ben, "Have you ever met her before?"

8. The teacher asked the pupils, "Are you ready? Can we start?"

9. Mr Miller wanted to know, "May I use your phone, please?"

10. Father asked, "Can you help me in the garden tomorrow afternoon?"

11. Ms Meyers asked the teacher, "Do you think that my son will pass the exam?"

12. Susan asked the policeman, "Where can I park my car?"

13. They asked the policeman, "Why is the road blocked? Has there been an accident?"

14. Jason asked his mum, "Can you give me a lift?"

15. Granny asked, "Where are my glasses? Has anyone seen them?"

16. The policeman asked the burglar, "How did you get into the house?"

17. Father wanted to know, "Why have you been so moody recently, Paul?"

18. The landlady asked her guests, "How did you sleep last night? Did you sleep well?"

19. Sue phoned Ann, "What are you doing at the moment? Have you already finished you essay?"

20. The man asked the secretary, "Can I speak to Mr Smith, please?"

21. Mary wanted to know, "Have you ever been to Canada?"

22. The doctor asked, "How many sleeping pills have you taken?"

23. The boss asked the secretary, "Where is Mr Blair? Have you already seen him today?"

24. Mr Jones wanted to know, "Are there any letters for me?"

25. The examiner asked, "For how long have you been learning English?"

Task 3: Reported Commands

Change into reported commands.

1. The teacher advised his students, "Study the Spanish grammar more exactly!"

2. The boss said to the secretary, "Post this letter for me, please!"

3. Pat said, "Let's go for a walk. It is not raining anymore!"

4. Mother said to her children, "Don't do any dangerous things!"

5. Father told his son, "Go and apply for the job!"

6. Peter advised Sue, "Don't lend Tim any money. He never pays back his debts."

7. The driving instructor ordered the learner driver, "Turn right at the next traffic light."

8. The policeman shouted at the burglar, "Hands up!"

9. Father said to me, "Remember to insure your luggage."

10. Mother said to Jill, "Don't forget to brush your teeth!"

11. Granny said to Betty, "Take your umbrella with you. I think it will be raining in the afternoon."

12. The stewardess said to the passengers, "Fasten your seatbelts, please."

13. Mum said to Tom, "Have your hair cut."

14. The driving instructor told the learner drivers, "Don't drink and drive!"

15. Mum advised Ann, "Get up earlier in the morning."

16. Father advised Tom, "Go to the dentist before your toothache gets worse."

17. Ann said, "Shut the window, please."

18. The mechanic told his apprentice, "Don't smoke in here!"

19. The policeman said to the driver, "Show me your driving license, please."

20. Mum said to me, "Sit down, please, and tell me what you are worried about."

21. Father said, "Let's go hiking tomorrow."

22. The lawyer advised his client, "Don't say anything else."

23. The judge ordered the accused, "Tell the truth, sir!"

24. The teacher told the pupils, "Please, remember to put your names at the top of the page."

25. Jill said, "Let's not tell anyone!"

Mother: "You stupid boy! Didn't I tell you to watch the saucepan and notice when it boiled over?"
Son: But I did, Mum. It was half past eleven."

Ziele erreicht? – Challenge 1: Change into reported speech

Change the following texts into reported speech.

 See 'Topics': Social Ties

What it is like to be a teenager in different countries

Disability

I cope well with my day-to-day life and like the fact that I go to a main-stream school. To some people it may seem that my disability is pretty serious and extremely hard to live with.

At the age of two I had both of my legs below the knee and part of my left arm amputated due to meningitis. To me it just seems normal and I feel lucky to only have that amount of disability.

The school I go to helps me to lead as normal a life as possible and get away from the fact that I have a disability. I can be with my friends and can take part in normal lessons. My school has lifts so I can access all classrooms easily. It's a bit tricky when people try to get a free ride on my wheel chair. My favourite lesson is P.E. If you think that's surprising, I recently competed in the national junior disability swimming championships and won two gold medals, one silver medal and beat two of my personal best times. My ambition is to swim in the Paralympics. At the moment I swim regionally for the North-East in the disability squad. The coaches are brilliant.

I walk on two prosthetic legs. I also have running blades which you may have seen athletes wearing at the Paralympics. I can run and keep up with my friends when we run around in the school yard.

Having my prosthetic limbs helps me because I can access my friends' homes, and when I go to a restaurant or to the local cricket club because I can just walk up and ask at the bar for a bag of crisps and a drink. When my legs are sore or tired and I can't use them, I use a wheelchair. I even pick up a lot of speed going downhill, it's all part of the fun!

BY WILL FROM NEWCASTLE, UK

War

In the morning when we open the window, we wish to see a view of peace, but we see the smoke of explosions, the shout of injured people, the sound of sadness and poverty and the buzz of attacks. But, while we were speaking with the children from the UK, we were not feeling like we were in Afghanistan because we had never thought one day we would be able to share with them with such friendly manner and with so much brotherhood. We understood that they were non-Muslims but again they empathised with our situation, and they expressed their sympathy saying we were very brave. Speaking with the children, we got some information about the UK, and the education system and school life there, which was very useful for us.

We came to appreciate the importance of unbiased behaviour, of friendship, sincerity and the taste of freedom and peace that the children in Afghanistan are looking forward to. We have  these words on our lips and are tirelessly repeating them. What we really appreciate is that even though we are different, we have some similarities such as having pets, hanging out with friends and playing instruments. It is really amazing how two sets of different nationalities get on together so well when they have never seen each other before.

BY MUHAMMAD, HAWA, HABIBULLA AND RAMZIA FROM KABUL, AFGHANISTAN

Violence

Singapore is a very safe country. The crime rates are low and I can go wherever I want to, without fear. Singapore is a sheltered and peaceful place. There are no conflicts overseas and no conflict at home. But the other thing about Singapore is the rules! The rule that irritates me the most is that chewing gum is illegal. I know that if I lived anywhere else I would not be able to do half of what I do now, to have the freedom to be so independent and move around without fear.

The main thing that bothers

me about Singapore is that there is very little that's exciting to do, especially for teenagers. There are a few places where you can go and have a good time but these places are only fun once. Furthermore, they cost a fortune and as a teenager I can't afford that all the time.

Maybe the grass is always greener on the other side of the fence. Singapore gives me a security and peace of mind that so many other children in the world don't have the good fortune to experience.

BY BEN FROM SINGAPORE

Disaster

When the earthquake started, I thought that it was the end of the world. When I went out I saw that everyone was crying for their family. In that moment, I thought of my family. I was imagining what happened to them because they were down-town at work. I grabbed my phone and tried to call my mum and my grandma.
When I saw my mum I asked her about my grandma. She said that a brick had broken her two feet. At 8 o'clock in

the evening, she died. My aunt knew that she was dead, but at first she didn't say anything to me. When I found out, I cried all the tears I could.
I'm still at school and people say I'm a little bit crazy but I know I'm not.

BY DYEANISE FROM HAITI

ALL: BBC ONLINE – ADAPTED

the grass is always greener on the other side of the fence =
die Kirschen in Nachbars Garten sind immer süßer

Little Jimmy told his mother that sardines were the stupidest fish in the world.
When she asked why he said that, he answered, "Well, they crawl into cans, lock themselves in, and leave the key on the outside."

 Ziele erreicht? – Challenge 2: Change into reported speech

First, read the text below.

 See 'Topics': Travelling and Tourism

Northern: Passenger reaction to rail firm being nationalised

The north of England's largest rail commuter service has been taken back into public ownership after years of poor performance. Northern passengers have endured delays, cancellations and overcrowding, with the transport secretary saying that people had lost trust in the rail network. The government announced it was terminating the existing franchise five years early and would take over the running of the service from 1 March. For many people who have faced repeated delays travelling on Northern trains, the news is welcomed.

Sam Barnes, 56, from Todmorden, West Yorkshire, said: "My brother-in-law is a train driver on London routes, and when he finishes his shift it takes him ages to get home on Northern as they are always delayed."

Passenger **Michael Ball** said, "Out of the 20 times I used Northern trains last week, only twice did they arrive on time. I'm glad it has been axed. It has never worked. The other day Northern got a kick up the arse from government, then the next day it was late again."

Manchester student **Martha High** said, "I'm all in favour of nationalisation. The government needs to ensure the new service is on time and affordable. I have had some bad experiences with Northern. Once I was waiting outside a station in a train for 45 minutes. Other times I have been waiting on my own in lonely Leeds stations on the Leeds line. It was pretty scary. When I was working before becoming a student my fare went up overnight from £2 to £12.50."

19-year-old engineering student **Faisal Hussein** said, "Once the service is brought under government control, I hope the situation will improve. I have missed lectures, and it is difficult to keep catching up with the course."

Olivia Dale, who had travelled from Pontefract to Leeds for a job interview, says, "Every train I have travelled on to get to the interview was delayed. It's shocking. I hope it gets better."

Janet Ulman, who arrived at Newcastle Central Station

from Sheffield, described the system as broken and said, "Northern is clearly not meeting customers' needs. It's unable to deliver, but it's part of a wider problem. I hope public ownership will improve things. A national rail service would be better again."

Her comments were echoed by passenger **Emma Finnigan**, from Darlington. She said, "Nationalisation is a good thing, but people should not lose their jobs, and existing workers' rights should be protected and looked after. That's really important."

However, there was some scepticism over whether the government could revive the franchise. **Andrew Smith**, from Dewsbury, said: "It's a bit harsh on Northern, they were running a service. I don't think a change will make a difference. It doesn't matter who does it, it's just the same."

BBC ONLINE – ADAPTED

Now report what the different passengers said by putting the underlined sentences into reported speech. Use a different verb at the beginning of each sentence.

- Sam Barnes said that ...
- Michael Ball added that ...
- Martha Hall explained that ...

etc.

Self-Check

✓ started ✓✓ on my way ✓✓✓ accomplished	✓	✓✓	✓✓✓
I can transfer sentences from direct to reported speech.			
I can form proper reported questions.			
I can build infinitive constructions to form correct reported commands.			
I can use all forms of reported speech appropriately in context.			

The Tenses

Die Zeitformen

 **Meine Ziele**

Nach Bearbeitung dieses Kapitels kann ich

■ die verschiedenen Zeiten und Zeitformen richtig bilden und anwenden;

■ alle Zeiten im Kontext entsprechend anwenden.

 **Task 1: Present Tense Simple or Continuous**

Fill in the correct forms of the verbs in brackets.

1. As Mary _____ (care) a lot about her health, she never _____ (buy) convenience food.

2. "Listen! Who _____ (sing) in the bathroom?

3. John is not satisfied with his job. He _____ (always, complain) about his boss, his colleagues and the working hours.

4. "I am tired. I _____ (go) to bed right now."

5. On weekends John normally _____ (meet) his best friend Matt. Both _____ (love) doing extreme sports like bungee jumping or rafting.

6. "Don't knock at her door. Mary _____ (prepare) some teaching materials for her Montessori lesson."

7. In the US the number of gun owners _____ (steadily, rise).

8. Although his girlfriend _____ (be) from Spain, Tom _____ (not, speak) Spanish very well.

9. "Where are Aaron and Maggie? What _____ (they, do)?" – "Aaron _____ (be) in the park and _____ (play) football with his friends. Maggie _____ (study) for her French test.

10. Sue normally _____ (do) her homework in the afternoon, but today she _____ (do) it in the evening.

11. The train _____ (leave) at 11.45.

12. The fact that smoking or chewing tobacco _____ (not, be) illegal and _____ (have) some social acceptance _____ (make) it harder to give up.

13. Every day the terkers _____ (punch) the clock when they _____ (arrive) at work.

14. "Oh, no! I have forgotten to turn off the light in the living room!" – "That's you all over! You _____ _____ (always, forget) something."

15. "Peter, _____ (not, cross) the street when the traffic light _____ (be) red!"

16. Adam _____ (be) a sportive person; he normally _____ (go) to university by bike, but today he _____ (take) the bus because it _____ (rain).

17. John _____ (not, be) lazy. Quite the contrary. He _____ (be) very ambitious and _____ (work) hard most of the time.

18. "What _____ (they, do)?" – "They _____ (think) about a catchy slogan for the new advertising campaign.

19. "The water _____ (boil). _____ (anybody, want) a cup of coffee?"

20. "How much _____ (you, earn) a month?" – "Why _____ _____ (you, want) to know that?"

21. "It _____ (rain). Can you lend me your umbrella?"

22. "Look! You have made the same mistake again!" – "Oh, no! I _____ (always, make) the same mistake."

23. "_____ (Tim, like) playing golf?" – "No, he _____ (not, like) golf at all. He _____ (prefer) slacklining."

24. "Be quiet! The baby _____ (sleep)!"

25. A disadvantage of tourism is that large numbers of tourists _____ (destroy) the landscape and _____ (pollute) the environment.

26. "Where _____ (you, live)? – I _____ (live) in London."

27. Figures _____ (show) that the number of people who _____ (be) overweight _____ (steadily, rise).

28. "What _____ (Luisa, do)?" – "She _____ (be) an architect, but she _____ (not, work) at the moment.

29. "_____ (you, listen) to the radio, Alan?" – "No, you can turn it off."

30. Rebecca _____ (be) very good at languages; she _____ (speak) three languages fluently.

31. While Rachel _____ (exercise) at the gym, her boyfriend Simon _____ (train) for athletics.

32. "What's wrong with Ralf? He _____ (not, seem) very happy." – "Well, don't you know? Alice broke up with him two days ago."

33. Mark normally _____ (not, wear) a suit to work; he usually _____ (wear) jeans and a T-Shirt. Today, however, they _____ (have) a meeting, and so he _____ (wear) a suit.

34. Jenny _____ (be) still in hospital. She has been in hospital for three weeks now, but she _____ (gradually, get) better.

35. "Are you ready, Carol?" – "Yes, I _____ (come)."

36. "What _____ (they, talk) about?" – "They _____ (talk) about tightening gun laws."

37. Mike _____ (love) horror movies but they _____ (not, interest) me at all.

38. "Why _____ (you, look) at me like that?"

39. Justin _____ (be) a very green person; therefore he _____ (cycle) to work whenever possible.

40. "You _____ (always, lose) your car keys. Why can't you put them at the same place?"

41. "Let's go for a walk now. The sun _____ (shine)."

42. "Hurry up! We _____ (wait) for you!"

43. Connie _____ (like) Physics, Chemistry and Biology; she always _____ (get) good marks in her science exams.

44. Normally I _____ (not, drink) any alcohol at lunchtime, but today I _____ (drink) a glass of wine because it is my birthday.

45. In summer it _____ (rain, never) much here. This summer, however, it _____ (rain) far more than usual.

46. These days, more and more people _____ (go) abroad for their holidays.

47. Mr Miller _____ (stay) with friends when he _____ (go) on business trips to Canada.

48. Macy usually _____ (study) in the library but, as the library _____ (be) closed today, she _____ (do) her studies at home.

49. Doctors _____ (not, understand) why the number of people who _____ (be) physically active _____ (constantly, decrease).

50. Fairtrade _____ (work) to improve opportunities for small-scale farmers and workers.

Ziele erreicht? – Challenge 1: Present Tense Simple or Continuous

Fill in the correct forms of the verbs in brackets.

 See 'Topics': Social Ties

What it is like to be a teenager in the UK II

Globalisation

I _____ (come) from Villiers High School in Southall West London and I _____ (want) to talk about how the future of young people could be affected by globalisation.

Globalisation _____ (mean) that the competition for the best jobs _____ (be) international. Nowadays so many countries _____ (create) young people with more talents, more skills, and more languages in the race for the best jobs.

The Prime Minister's Global Fellowship _____ (be) a project which _____ (allow) 100 young people from different backgrounds and schools to experience life in Brazil, China or India. They _____ (have) a chance to discover what globalisation _____

_____ (stand) for and what the impact will be on the young people of the UK.

We contacted two 'Global Fellows' who went to China. One of them, Chelsea, explained what globalisation means and told us about her six weeks in China. Now she _____ (learn) Mandarin at university as a result of her trip.

The big multinational companies _____ (expand) and _____ (set) up businesses all over the world. Speaking English _____ (be) no big deal any more. If you _____ (be) able to do deals in Mandarin, Russian, or Japanese, then you _____ (take) part in the competition.

BY NITESH FROM LONDON, UK
BBC ONLINE – ADAPTED

A man walks into a pub with a front door under his arm.
The barman asks him, "Why are you carrying that door?" –
"Well," says the Irishman, "last night I lost the key, so in any case anybody finds it and breaks into my house I am carrying the door around." –
"But what happens if you leave the door somewhere?"
"That's OK," says the Irishman, "I have left a window open."

Task 2: *Will, Going-to* Present Continuous

Fill in the correct forms of the verbs in brackets.

1. Mother expects that her children _____ (be) at home for lunch.

2. "Where _____ (you, spend) your summer holidays?" – "We _____ (stay) at a luxury green hotel in the south of Spain."

3. Justin Bieber _____ (arrive) at London Heathrow Airport at 9 pm.

4. As the number of young people who are unemployed _____ (steadily, rise)

    governments _____ (have) to think about measure to tackle the problem.

5. Scientists predict that there _____ (be) more droughts and forest fires.

6. Jason _____ (see) his boss tomorrow morning.

7. As exhaust fumes from motorised vehicles contribute greatly to environmental pollution, experts _____

    _____ (think) about environmentally friendlier means of transport.

8. In 50 years' time people _____ (go) on holiday to space.

9. The internet _____ (force) its way into every aspect of people's lives.

10. Sue hopes that the weather _____ (be) sunny and warm tomorrow.

11. "Look, all the people _____ (leave)."

12. Experts are worried that the increase in obesity _____ (lead) to more health problems such as

    Type II diabetes; it is said that the number of people with diabetes _____ (double) within the next

    ten years.

13. "What _____ (you, do) next weekend?" – Well, if the weather is fine, Patrick and I

    _____ (go) bungee jumping."

14. "Do you worry that Tom _____ (not, pass) the Apprenticeship Diploma?" – "No, I

    think he _____ (do) it quite well."

15. "Look at those black clouds! It _____ (rain) in a few minutes."

16. As soon as Jason is back, they _____ (have) lunch.

17. As the world population _____ (constantly, rise), experts believe that there

    _____ (be) more than 9 billion people living in urban centres by 2050. Therefore competition for

    land to grow both food and energy crops _____ (become) increasingly fierce.

18. Peter thinks that in the future computers _____ (replace) teachers and that there probably

    _____ (be, not) any schools anymore.

19. "What _____ (do) with that ladder?" – "I _____ (have) a look on the roof

    because it is leaking."

20. "I wonder if Paul knows that the time of the meeting has been changed." – "Probably not. I _____

    (call) him right now."

21. Due to the financial crisis many companies _____ (dismiss) staff.

22. The Department of Sociology at Oxford University has found out that mothers _____ (continue)

    to carry the burden of childcare and housework for the next four decades.

23. When Sue has finished doing the washing up, she _____ (meet) her friend Pamela.

24. More and more people _____ (leave) the countryside in order to live in the city.

25. They _____ (decorate) the house for Christmas on Sunday.

26. The boys _____ (play) football this afternoon.

27. The Millers _____ (leave) for Canada tomorrow morning.

28. "When I am 18 I _____ (do) my driving license."

29. There _____ (be) a meeting for the staff next Friday.

30. When Tim gets to Boston next week he _____ (stay) with friends.

31. As Tom is very fond of limbo skating he _____ (buy) new roller skates tomorrow.

32. "_____ (you, watch) TV this evening?" – "Well, I don't know."

33. Father _____ (be) 50 tomorrow.

34. Mother hopes that Sue _____ (call) soon.

35. "Where _____ (Alan, go) for his next holidays?" – "I do not know; probably he _____ (do) an adventure holiday."

36. "Do you think we _____ (see) Jason tomorrow?" – "I hope so. He _____ (probably, look) in on his way to the train station."

37. Unfortunately, Simon _____ (go) to the party tonight.

38. Hopefully the pupils _____ (do) better the next time.

39. Sue and Adam _____ (see) to their bank manager tomorrow.

40. Some people believe that one day there _____ (be) one world language.

41. "We would better leave a message for Mum. Otherwise she _____ (not, know) where we have gone and she _____ (be) worried."

42. "We _____ (have) a party next Saturday. Would you like to come?"

43. "Oh, no! We have run out of coffee!" – "I _____ (go) and buy some."

44. "Have you recently seen Simon?" – "No, but I _____ (see) him on Friday."

45. The children promise that they _____ (not, lie) to their parents again.

46. John _____ (meet) Paula at the cinema this evening.

47. "Look at that ship! It _____ (hit) the rocks!"

48. In 2150 there _____ (be) day trips to the moon.

49. "I still haven't got your project!" – "I _____ (hand) it in on Friday, I promise."

50. When I am grown up I _____ (have) a big house with a garden. I _____ (probably, be) married and have two children.

to leak = undicht sein

Headmaster: "From now on there will be no more physical punishment in this school."

Pupil: "Does that mean there will be no more school lunches?"

 ## Task 3: Past Tense Simple or Continuous

Fill in the correct forms of the verbs in brackets.

1. The taxi _____ (arrive) when Alan _____ (have) breakfast.

2. When I _____ (wake) up yesterday morning, the sun _____ (shine) through the window.

3. "_____ (you, be) at work last week?" – "Last week I _____ _____ (not, go) to work because I _____ (be) ill. I _____ (have) a terrible cold and I _____ (have) to stay in bed.

4. Yesterday she _____ (sleep) all day long because she _____ (not, feel) fine.

5. This time last year, the Ann and Chris _____ (study) for their A-levels.

6. When I _____ (look) for my passport, I _____ (find) that old photograph.

7. He _____ (clean) his revolver, when it accidentally _____ (go) off and _____ (kill) him.

8. As I _____ (cross) the street I _____ (step) on a banana skin and _____ (fall) heavily. I _____ (still, lie) on the street when I saw a lorry approaching. Luckily, the lorry driver _____ (see) me and _____ (stop) the lorry in time.

9. Yesterday afternoon the children _____ (swim) in the swimming pool.

10. What _____ (they, do) last weekend at this time? – They _____ (have) a party. They _____ (have) fun, _____ (dance), _____ (talk) and _____ (laugh) all night long.

11. When I _____ (read) the newspaper, the telephone suddenly _____ (ring).

12. As Jim _____ (walk) down the street, a dog suddenly _____ (attack) him.

13. What _____ (you, do) when I _____ (call) you this morning? – I _____ (do) the washing up.

14. The baby _____ (cry) all morning long.

15. It _____ (rain) heavily when he _____ (leave) the house.

16. When _____ (you, buy) your house? – Well, let me think. I _____ (buy) it in 2003.

17. He _____ (understand) exactly what I _____ (want) to say.

18. The film _____ (not, be) very good. I _____ (not, enjoy) it very much.

19. I _____ (meet) Tom at the airport some weeks ago. While we _____ (wait) to board our planes, we _____ (sit) in the café and _____ (talk) about the good old days.

20. Tom _____ (burn) his hand when he _____ (cook) dinner.

21. While Jim _____ (listen) to the radio, Pam _____ (read) a book. Suddenly the doorbell _____ (ring). So Pam _____ (stand) up and _____ (go) downstairs to open the door. It _____ (be) Tom, who _____ (want) to know if Jim _____ (be) at home.

22. When Tim _____ (be) a child, he _____ (love) playing table tennis.

23. I have not seen Jason for ages. When I last _____ (see) him, he _____ (look) for a job.

24. "Why _____ (you, not, tell) Joe that Tom had been here?" – "I'm sorry, but I _____ (forget) because I _____ (be) so busy. I _____ (have) so much work to do: all afternoon long I _____ (work) in the garden."

25. When Jason was a young man in his twenties he _____ (use) to do extreme sports like cliff diving, underwater hockey or bungee jumping on weekends.

26. Last Monday the students _____ (talk) about McDonald's new advertising campaign, which emphasises the new healthy Happy Meal, with low fat milk, fewer fries and apple slices.

27. Yesterday Johnny _____ (go) to school by bike, but he _____ (not, see) the dog in front of him and _____ (fall) off. Some boys _____ (hear) the noise and _____ (run) to help him. They _____ (find) him on the pavement and _____ (help) him. Luckily he _____ (not, be) severely injured. He _____ (not, have) to be taken to hospital.

28. "_____ (you, help) Sandy cleaning her room?" – "Yes, I _____ (do). She _____ (ask) me for help and as I _____ (have) time I _____ (change) the bed linen."

29. This time last August Jill and Thomas _____ (leave) for their 'Best-of-the-Rockies' tour. They _____ (do) a 17-day adventure trip: after leaving Seattle, they _____ (drive) a short distance west to Olympic National Park. They _____ (spend) a whole day there; they _____ (stroll) through the Hoh Rainforest and _____ (relax) in Sol Hot Springs. The next day they _____ (visit) the Craters of the Moon National Monument, which is a volcanic area where NASA's Apollo astronauts _____ (use) to do some of their training. Yellowstone National Park, which is home to a large variety of wildlife, _____ (be) their next destination. Unfortunately, they _____ (not, see) any of the wildlife. Their next stop _____ (be) Montana Lodge, an authentic working guest ranch. While Jill _____ (enjoy) a horseback ride, Thomas _____ (help) to prepare an old-fashioned cowboy

meal. They _____ (continue) to Jasper National Park where they _____ (take) the cable car to Whistler Mountain. In the afternoon Thomas _____ (go) mountain biking while Jill _____ (visit) Mount Edith Cavell.

Their 'Best-of-the-Rockies' tour _____ (end) in Vancouver. As Jill and Thomas really _____ (enjoy) their tour, they _____ (decide) to do the Costa Rica Panama Trail this year.

30. Power plants that are not constructed and maintained properly can create disasters. Chernobyl _____ (be) a nuclear power plant in the former Soviet Union. In April 1986 it _____ (suffer) a massive failure; the reactor at Chernobyl _____ (blow) up, and radioactive dust _____ (contaminate) large parts of Europe.

31. Television is one of the few inventions that _____ (changed, truly) the world. It _____ (be) the key to delivering images to whole nations and indeed the whole world as they _____ (happen). It _____ (be) the first technology that allowed many people to see and experience events that _____ (be) hundreds or thousands of miles away. Television _____ (provide) low cost entertainment. Before television, theatre _____ (be) the main form of entertainment. Television _____ (bring) entertainment right into the home and it _____ (make) entertainment a passive activity. Television has changed home life dramatically. In the early part of the 20th century, the home _____ (be) centred around a kitchen or around a dining table, the two places where a family got together. The television _____ (make) its way into the centre of the family and now takes centre stage in the living room.

Father: "What happened to that shockproof, unbreakable, antimagnetic watch I gave you for your birthday?"
Son: "I lost it last week."

Task 4: Past or Past Perfect, Simple or Continuous

Fill in the correct forms of the verbs in brackets.

1. Susan went to Michael's flat, but he was not there. He _____ (go out).

2. I invited Nick to the party, but he could not come because he _____ (book) a flight to Tokyo.

3. I was very happy to see her after such a long time. I _____ (not, see) her for seven years.

4. When Fred _____ (arrive) the match _____ (already, begin).

5. He invited me for lunch, but I was not hungry. I _____ (have) a late breakfast.

6. Tom _____ (not, know) the word because he _____ (not, use) a dictionary.

7. Twenty years after the A-levels we went back to our school, but we hardly recognised the building. It _____ (change) a lot.

8. Ms Miller _____ (tell) the police that she _____ (never, see) that man before.

9. After John _____ (win) in the lottery, he _____ (buy) a Ferrari.

10. He _____ (tell) us that he _____ (be) on holidays in Spain last week.

11. Mary _____ (live) in a big city until she and her husband _____ (move) here.

12. Before they _____ (go) on holiday they _____ (book) the flight.

13. Mother _____ (watch) a video after her children _____ (go) to bed.

14. Granny _____ (not, tell) us that she _____ (be) ill last week.

15. The travel agent _____ (recommend) the couple the hotel which _____ (be) renovated last March.

16. Jason _____ (play) in a football team until he _____ (hurt) his knee.

17. Peter _____ (work) at IBM for twelve years before he _____ (quit).

18. We _____ (just, start) when they _____ (arrive).

19. The week before Alan _____ (have) his final exam he _____ (study) a lot.

20. Pat _____ (want) to wear the trousers his mum _____ (just, wash).

21. When Jason _____ (leave) for the office that morning he was not feeling very awake because he _____ (not, sleep) very well.

22. Mother _____ (be) very angry with Ann because she _____ (not, call) her.

23. The room _____ (look) like new after Bill _____ (paint) it.

24. When I _____ (get) to school I _____ (find) out that I _____ (forget) my homework.

25. After the students _____ (do) the experiment, they _____ (write) a report on it.

26. After the festival the park _____ (look) awful because people _____ (leave) litter everywhere.

27. There _____ (be) no sign of a taxi although I _____ (order) one half an hour before.

28. Alice _____ (call) her dad at work before she _____ (leave) for the trip.

29. The chairmen _____ (not, speak) until he _____ (hear) all the arguments.

30. Pat _____ (go) to the dentist this morning because his tooth _____ (ache).

31. The grass _____ (be) yellow because it _____ (not, rain) the whole summer.

32. Some children _____ (start) a house fire because they _____ (play) with matches.

33. As I _____ (see) the film before I _____ (not, go) to the cinema with Sue and Pat.

34. After Peter _____ (spend) his holiday in Spain he _____ (want) to learn Spanish.

35. When Granny _____ (try) to call us, we _____ (already, leave) the house.

36. After President Trump _____ (finish) his speech he _____ (be) asked a lot questions by the journalists.

37. On my first day at the driving school I _____ (be) quite nervous because I _____ (not, drive) a car before.

38. As it _____ (be) a cold and rainy Sunday afternoon Alice _____ (decide) to finish her essay she _____ (start) writing a few days before.

39. The secretary _____ (send) the email that she _____ (just, write).

40. When Fred _____ (come) home he _____ (see) that someone _____ (break) into his house. After he _____ (call) the police they _____ (look) around and _____ (notice) that Fred _____ (not, lock) the bathroom window.

Little Millie: "I wish I had been born a hundred years earlier."
Mother: "Why, Millie?"
Little Millie: "Well, you would not dare to tell a little old lady to tidy up her room."

Task 5: Past or Present Perfect, Simple or Continuous

Fill in the correct forms of the verbs in brackets.

1. Tim _____ (have) to go to the dentist's yesterday.

2. "I don't know where Ann is. _____ (you, see) her?" – "Well, when I _____ (see) her about an hour ago; she _____ (work) on her presentation."

3. What _____ (they, do) this time on Sunday? – John _____ (play) table tennis with his friend Jason and Sue _____ (chat) on the phone with her cousin Pam.

4. _____ (the students, already, read) 'About a Boy' by Nick Hornby? – Yes, of course.

They already _____ (finish) reading yesterday. Since then they _____ (work)

on their presentation."

5. The Chinese _____ (invent) printing.

6. "What do you think of my French? Do you think I _____ (improve)?" – "Yes, certainly."

7. George _____ (leave) school three years ago. Since then he _____ (study)

International Business in Vienna.

8. Tom is very hungry. He _____ (not, eat) anything since breakfast.

9. Your car looks very clean. _____ (you, wash) it?

10. Rose _____ (give) up smoking last year. So she _____ (not,

smoke) for one year.

11. Is Mr Smith still here? – No, unfortunately not. He _____ (just, leave) the office.

12. Sue and Pam _____ (know) each other for a long time. They first _____

(meet) at university and _____ (be) friends ever since.

13. Tim _____ (have) a dog for three months now.

14. Since when _____ (Jim, be) back from Spain? – He _____

(come) back two days ago.

15. Are you thirsty? – No, thanks. I _____ (just, have) a drink.

16. Last week Paul _____ (be) at Tim's birthday party but I _____

(not, see) him since then.

17. Mother _____ (wash) her hair. It is still wet.

18. In 2010 John _____ (visit) London for the first time. From the first moment on he _____

_____ (feel) at home and _____ (decide) to work and live in this fascinating cosmopolitan

city. In spring 2011 John _____ (move) to London and _____ (live) there ever

since.

19. "What are you going to do this afternoon?" – "As soon as I _____ (finish) writing the essay I will

meet Bill and Aaron in the park to train for the slacklining competition next Saturday."

20. Unfortunately, I _____ (not, be) at home when she _____ (call)

yesterday evening.

21. As Tim _____ (not, feel) fine yesterday he _____ (stay) in bed all

day long.

22. When the police _____ (stop) the Miller's car for a routine check, they _____

(realise) that he _____ (be) the man who had robbed the bank.

23. This diagram shows how the climate _____ (change).

24. When we _____ (do) the English test, the fire alarm _____ (go) off.

25. This time last year I _____ (do) my final exam.

26. "_____ (you, ever, be) to a ghost town in the American West?" – "Last summer

my family and I _____ (go) to California; one day we _____ (visit) the ghost

town of Bodie, an abandoned mining town in the northeast." – "And? How _____ (be) it?" –

"Unfortunately, Bodie _____ (be) nearly completely destroyed by a big fire in the 1930s, but what

_____ (be) spared by the fire still stands today. So we _____ (stroll) around

the town: we _____ (go) inside the church and the fire house, we _____

(have) a look into the school house and finally we _____ (have) a drink in the saloon."

27. "Why are you crying?" – "Because my brother _____ (have) an accident."

28. "_____ (you, see) the news on TV last night?" – "No, I _____

_____ (not, have) any time to watch TV because I _____ (have) so much work to do."

29. I _____ (work) for that company for twenty years.

30. "Do you know how Tim is doing? When I last _____ (see) him he _____

(look) for a job." – "Well, Tim is fine. I _____ (meet) him at Starbucks yesterday morning. Since

May this year he _____ (work) for Interpublic, one the largest advertising companies in the world."

31. I _____ (learn) Spanish for eight years now.

32. "I'm sorry to keep you waiting. I hope you _____ (not, wait) long.

33. "Please drive carefully to work. It _____ (snow) and the roads are very slippery."

34. Pam _____ (live) in Brighton since she _____ (get) married.

35. "Excuse me. Whose is this bag? Who _____ (leave) it here?" – "I don't know. I _____

_____ (sit) here all afternoon, but I _____ (not, notice) it until now."

36. Jason is a very sporty person. When he _____ (be) a child he _____ (use)

to play football and tennis. As a teenager he _____ (love) to do more extreme sports like air

kicking or bungee jumping. One day his best friend Alan _____ (tell) him about Parkour, a system

of different movements designed to help a person to surmount whatever lies in his path. From the first day on,

Jason _____ (be) fascinated by this sport and _____ (train) every day ever

since. Unfortunately, Jason _____ (break) his leg last Saturday So he _____

_____ (not, be) able to do Parkour for six days now.

37. Television _____ (be) one of the most influential inventions of the 20th century. Since the late

1920s the TV set _____ (become) commonplace in homes, businesses and companies.

38. In 1983 Motorola _____ (release) the first commercially available mobile phone. Since then,

mobile phones _____ (change) from being rare and expensive means of communication to

being a must-have everyday personal item. They _____ (become) a crucial part of our daily life

nowadays.

39. People _____ (keep) in touch via text messages ever since they _____ (be)

commercially introduced in 1995. In 2012 the International Telecommunications Union _____

(report) that 200,000 text messages _____ (be) sent every minute.

40. In 1776, the United States _____ (become) independent from the British Crown. The constitution _____ (be) written by Thomas Jefferson in 1787 and _____ (remain) unchanged since that time.

Ziele erreicht? – Challenge 2: Past Tenses: Past – Present Perfect (Simple and Continuous)

Fill in the correct forms of the verbs in brackets.

 See 'Topics': English around the World

Saint Patrick's Day in Britain

Irish tourism chiefs _____ (ask) the Queen for the green light for a Saint Patrick's Day favour. They want the monarch to turn Buckingham Palace emerald on the Irish national saint's day. Some of world's most famous sights, including the Pyramids and Rio de Janeiro's Christ the Redeemer statue, will be going green on March 17.

The Queen _____ (give, not yet) permission for a changing of the colour at her official London residence. (If she does, the result might look a little like this computer mock-up.)

Niall Gibbons, chief executive of Tourism Ireland, said they _____ (await, still) a response from Buckingham Palace. "We _____ (have, not) a reply from the private secretary to the Queen yet," he said. "I _____ (write) a couple of months ago, but it is a dialogue that is in progress."

Other international attractions going green on March 17 include the Sydney Opera House, Niagara Falls, the Leaning Tower of Pisa, Burj al Arab in Dubai, Table Mountain in South Africa, New York's Empire State Building and Berlin's TV Tower.

The entire scheme, which will also see the 'greening' of New Zealand's Sky Tower, Vienna's Burg Theatre and the Prince's Palace in Monaco, is costing about 34,000 euros (£ 29,400). Ireland is turning to its strong identity abroad to help lift it out of an unprecedented economic crash.

Tourism Ireland _____ (hope) that the visit of the Queen and Duke of Edinburgh to Ireland some years ago, which had been the first by a British monarch to the Republic since independence, would prompt a rise in the number of holidaymakers from the UK. However, figures _____ (be, so far) disappointing, with visitor numbers down 3 % last year.

"The British market is very difficult," Mr Varadkar, the Irish Republic's tourism minister, _____ (say). "Fewer British people _____ (travel) abroad last year than 15 years ago, and a lot of people still believe that Ireland is an expensive place to visit.

Fortunately, all the research we _____ (do) recently shows that this is improving, and British people now coming to Ireland are going back and saying that Ireland isn't that expensive after all and that hotels and accommodation in particular are very good value. However, it will take a bit of time for that to filter through."

BBC Online – Adapted

Son: "Dad, I took apart your car and put it back together again."
Father: "I hope you haven't lost any bit."
Son: "No, I actually have got seven bits left over."

Ziele erreicht? – Challenge 3: Past Tenses: Past – Present Perfect – Past Perfect

Fill in the correct forms of the verbs in brackets (simple forms only).

See 'Topics': Globalisation and International Trade

Scotland meets Fair Trade standards

Scotland _____ _____ (become) a Fair Trade Nation after achieving its target of having all six cities and 18 of its 32 councils acquiring fair trade status. Scottish Fair Trade Forum director Martin Rhodes _____ (welcome) the news that it _____ (follow) Wales in becoming one of the first nations to have the Fair Trade status.

Fair Trade products are said to offer a better deal to workers in developing countries. Mr Rhodes said it _____ (have) a positive impact on their lives and their communities. "Fair Trade premiums paid to producers _____ (enable) them to enjoy higher and more stable incomes, especially when global prices _____ (be) low," he suggested.

The remarks _____ (come) as Humza Yousaf, the Minister for External Relations and International Development, formally _____ (announce) that Scotland had met the criteria. Mr Rhodes _____ (add), "Fair Trade Nation status is a celebration of what we _____ (achieve) and a platform to campaign for further change in global trade. It marks the success of the partnership between producers in the developing world and consumers and campaigners here in Scotland. While we have much to celebrate today, work must continue to further embed Fair Trade values across all sectors of society."

By February 62 Scottish towns _____ (acquire) Fairtrade status, and almost two-thirds of higher education institutions and 171 schools _____ (achieve) the standard.

BBC Online – Adapted

Task 6: Mixed Tenses – All Forms and Tenses

Fill in the correct forms of the verbs in brackets.

1. "Look! A spider _____ (climb) up the wall."

2. While father _____ (do) the washing up, mother _____ (work) in the garden.

3. "_____ (you, ever, be) to New York?" – "Yes, I _____ (be) there last August."

4. I hope the weather _____ (be) fine tomorrow.

5. Sue _____ (do) her homework, when the doorbell _____ (ring). She _____ (stand) up, _____ (go) downstairs and _____ (open) the door.

6. The students _____ (have) an English exam tomorrow. Therefore they _____ (study) a lot since last week.

7. After Tom _____ (finish) his homework, he _____ (go) to the cinema with his friends.

8. At the moment the students _____ (listen) to their teacher who _____ (talk) about graphs and charts for 10 minutes.

9. Ben and Jenny _____ (move) to Australia in 2011. They _____ (live) in Sydney ever since.

10. When they _____ (watch) TV, the telephone _____ (ring).

11. Granny _____ (be) 80 next week.

12. "What _____ (do) in your holidays?" – "Well, we _____ (not, know). I _____ (not, want) to go to Italy again as we _____ (be) there last year. I _____ (want) to go to Sweden or Norway but the children _____ (love) swimming in the sea and playing on the beach. They really _____ (enjoy) it last year. Therefore we _____ (not, make) up our minds yet, but I hope that we _____ (can decide) on a destination the following weekend."

13. The Millers _____ (buy) a new house last summer, but they _____ (not, sell) the old house yet.

14. I promise that I _____ (not, tell) anybody about the accident.

15. "What time _____ (train, leave)?" – "It usually _____ (leave) at 6.30, but today it _____ (leave) 10 minutes later."

16. When we _____ (play) tennis it suddenly _____ (start) to rain.

17. The dancing club _____ (have) its summer party in July.

18. Mother expects that her children _____ (be) at home for lunch.

19. Sue _____ (already, finish) her work when Jim _____ (call).

20. Granny _____ (not, tell) us that she _____ (be) ill last week.

21. The secretary _____ (just, finish) writing the letters.

22. When I _____ (come) home yesterday, he _____ (sit) in his armchair, asleep.

23. "Since when _____ (you, have) your new bike?" – "I _____ (buy) it last Saturday."

24. Jason _____ (tell) the police that there _____ (be) an accident in Park Avenue.

25. "_____ (you, speak) to my sister yesterday?" – "No, I _____ (not, see) her for a long time. I cannot remember when I last _____ (see) her."

26. "Do you think your team _____ (win) this match?" – "Yes, of course. Last month we _____ (win) six out of eight matches."

27. The Prime Minister _____ (arrive) at 9 am at the Vienna International Airport.

28. Scientists predict that due to the global warming the polar caps and glaciers _____ (melt). As a consequence the sea level _____ (rise), leading to the flooding of large coastal areas.

29. "I _____ (lose) my keys. _____ (you, see) them?" – "No, I _____ (not, see) them, but I _____ (help) you in about five minutes. I _____ (want) to finish homework first."

30. Last Saturday there _____ (be) Alan's summer party. I _____ (enjoy) it a lot. Unfortunately Peter _____ (come) very late. So when he _____ (arrive), I _____ (already, go). I _____ (be) really disappointed because I _____ (not, see) him for months.

31. Last Monday the students _____ (talk) about McDonald's new advertising campaign which _____ (emphasise) the new health Happy Meal, with low fat milk, fewer fries and apple slices.

32. By 2050 nearly 80 % of the global population _____ (live) in urban centres. An estimated 10 billion hectares of new land _____ (be) needed to grow enough food to feed them.

33. The most commonly used data application on mobile phones _____ (be) text messaging. Billions _____ (be) sent over the world every day. People _____ (keep) in touch via text messages ever since they _____ (be) commercially introduced in 1995.

34. Social Networking _____ (be) one of the leading means of communication of all times that _____ (revolutionise) the way people associate with one another. When the Web's first social network site _____ (be) founded in 1994, no one expected the internet world would one day evolve and become what it _____ (be) today: the largest virtual community which _____ (enable) people all around the globe to share information and ideas, to connect in a matter of seconds and interact by just a few keystrokes.

35. The family in Britain _____ (change). The once typical British family headed by

two parents _____ (undergo) substantial changes during the twentieth century. In

particular there _____ (be) a rise in the number of single-person households, which

_____ (increase) from 18 to 29 per cent of all households between 1971 and 2002.

By the year 2030, it _____ (be) estimated that there _____

_____ (be) more single people than married people. Fifty years ago this would have been socially unacceptable

in Britain.

In the past, people _____ (get) married and _____

(stay) married. Divorce _____ (be) very difficult, expensive and _____

_____ (take) a long time. Today, people's views on marriage _____

_____ (change). Many couples, mostly in their twenties or thirties, _____

(live) together without getting married. Only about 60 % of these couples _____

(get, eventually) married.

🎯 Ziele erreicht? – Challenge 4: Mixed Tenses – All Forms and Tenses

Fill in the correct forms of the verbs in brackets.   🔗 See 'Topics': Learning and Education

Is an apprenticeship valued enough?

**Is going to university better than doing a vocational qualification or an apprenticeship?
We asked three people their views.**

For years the experts _____ (tell) us that if you want to get on in life and be successful then you have to go to university, and manual work _____ (be) only for those who are not clever enough to make it to university. And where _____ (get, that) us? Thousands of useless courses and hundreds of thousands of students with huge debts and no jobs, that's where.

After ranting about this for years, it _____ (seem) I'm not alone here any more. In her report on vocational education, Professor Alison Wolf _____

_____ (come) to the conclusion that the government _____ (help) to downgrade jobs like plumbing, carpentry, electrics – you know, the useful ones in society – in social status over the years, a situation that must be changed if we _____ (want) to solve the huge youth unemployment problem.

One step forward might be to stop using terms like vocational. We should be talking about 'getting a trade', something many parents used to aim to for their kids in the 1970s.

CHARLIE MULLINS, MD OF PIMLICO PLUMBERS

to rant = meckern
MD = Managing Director

The government _____ (invest) heavily in creating new apprenticeships. At the same time, it _____ (introduce) the EBacc, which _____ (focuse) solely on academic qualifications. What _____ (miss) is an alternative, a technical baccalaureate, which offers valuable learning and real skills, and leads to real jobs for young people.

Critics might say that encouraging children down one pathway at 14 _____ (be) questionable. Our experience _____ (show) that getting children on the right programme for their learning needs is what _____ (lead) to success.

GILL WORGAN, PRINCIPAL OF WEST HERTS COLLEGE

Vocational qualifications definitely _____ (appear) to be more attractive now that big companies such as BAE Systems _____ (offer) apprenticeships, but I would only consider that route if I didn't get the grades I needed for university.

Given the choice, I would definitely go for A-levels, as I _____ (think) they _____ (be) far more respected by employers and universities.

EWAN WRIGHT, YEAR 10 STUDENT AT HIGHLANDS SCHOOL IN ENFIELD

ALL: GUARDIAN.CO.UK – ADAPTED

EBacc = The English Baccalaureate (known as the EBacc) is a performance measure which recognises the achievement of GCSEs at Grades A* to C in five subject areas.

Ziele erreicht? – Super-Challenge: Mixed Tenses

Fill in the correct forms of the verbs in brackets.

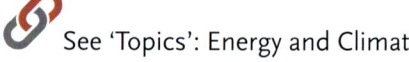

See 'Topics': Energy and Climate

Extreme and unusual climate trends continue after record 2016

In the atmosphere, the seas and around the poles, climate change _____ (reach) disturbing new levels across the Earth. That's according to a detailed global analysis from the World Meteorological Organization (WMO). It says that 2016 _____ (be) not only the warmest year on record, but it saw atmospheric CO2 rise to a new high, while Arctic sea ice recorded a new winter low. The "extreme and unusual" conditions _____ (continue) since 2016, it says.

Reports earlier this year from major scientific bodies – including the UK's Met Office, Nasa and NOAA – indicated that 2016 was the warmest year on record. The WMO's State of the Global Climate 2016 report _____ (build) on this research with information from 80 national weather services to provide a deeper and more complete picture of the year's climate data.

Compared with the 1961–1990 reference period, 2016 _____ (be) 0.83 degrees C warmer than the average. It was around 1.1C above the pre-industrial period, and at 0.06C just a fraction warmer than the previous warmest year record in 2015. "This increase in global temperature is consistent with other changes occurring in the climate system," said WMO Secretary-General, Petteri Taalas. "Globally averaged sea-surface temperatures _____ (be) also the warmest on record, global sea-levels continued to rise, and Arctic sea-ice extent was well below average for most of the year," he said.

Not all the world _____ (warm) at equal speed in 2016. In the Arctic, temperatures were about 3 degrees C above the 1961–1990 average. In Svalbard, the Norwegian island high in the Arctic circle, the yearly average was 6.5 degrees above the long-term mark. The report _____ (say) that temperatures in 2016 were "substantially influenced" by the El Niño weather phenomenon, contributing 0.1 to 0.2 degrees on top of the longer-term warming driven by emissions of CO2.

However, El Niño also _____ (have) an influence on the levels of the gas in the atmosphere. "The CO2 rise in 2016 was the fastest on record – 3.4ppm (parts per million) per year – because the El Niño weakened the tropical carbon sink and _____ (give) the ongoing CO2 rise an extra kick on top of the effect of human emissions," said Prof Richard Betts from the Met Office Hadley Centre. "As a result, 2016 _____ (become) the first year in which CO2 measurements at Mauna Loa remained above 400ppm all year round."

The report _____ (state) that extreme weather events in 2016 included severe droughts in southern and eastern Africa, and in Central America. Hurricane Matthew in the North Atlantic _____ (be) one of the most damaging weather-related disasters, leaving hundreds of dead and swathes of destruction across Haiti.

The WMO says that the "extreme and unusual" climate and weather trends _____ (continue).

At least three times this winter, the Arctic experienced the equivalent of a heatwave, as powerful Atlantic storms _____ (drive) warm, moist air into the region.

Changes in the Arctic and the melting of sea-ice are also leading to a shift in atmospheric circulation patterns impacting other parts of the world. This _____ (cause) unusual heat in some areas – In the US, over 11,000 warm temperature records were broken in early 2017.

"Even without a strong El Niño, we _____ (see) other remarkable changes across the planet that are challenging the limits of our understanding of the climate system. We are now in truly uncharted territory," said David Carlson, World Climate Research Programme Director at the WMO.

In the face of all this information, climate researchers around the world are irritated by the attitude of the Trump government in Washington. The new administration _____ (roll) back some of the global warming measures taken by President Obama, while the newly appointed head of the Environmental Protection Agency, Scott Pruitt, _____ (deny) that CO2 was a primary contributor to warming.

"The WMO's statement on the 2016 climate _____ (leave) no room for doubt. The much-hyped warming hiatus is over – and the 'missing' heat energy didn't go missing at all. Instead, that heat went into the ocean, and we _____ (get) much of it back again last year," said Dr Phil Williamson, from the University of East Anglia. "Human-driven climate change is now an empirically verifiable fact, combining year-to-year variability with the consequences of our release of extra greenhouse gases. Those who dispute that link are not sceptics, but anti-science deniers."

BBC ONLINE – ADAPTED

Self-Check

✓ started   ✓✓ on my way   ✓✓✓ accomplished

	✓	✓✓	✓✓✓
I can build the different tenses and forms correctly.			
I can use all present, past and future tenses in their simple and continuous forms in sentences.			
I can use all tenses appropriately in context.			

The Word Order

Die Wortstellung im Satz

 **Meine Ziele**

Nach Bearbeitung dieses Kapitels kann ich

- die verschiedenen Umstandsangaben in der korrekten Reihenfolge im Satz anordnen;
- Umstandswörter der Häufigkeit und ähnliche Adverbien an die richtige Stelle im Satz setzen.

 **Task: Word Order**

Form meaningful sentences by putting the words into a suitable order.

1. a pair of jeans | Ann | yesterday | bought

2. went skiing | to France | last winter | they

3. Ben and Jill | at a speed-dating event | met | some months ago

4. can be opened | this door lock | by a burglar | easily

5. at home | usually | is | Mr Miller | in the evening

6. would | again | never | to her | Nick | lie

7. the wonderful holiday | Ann | in Spain | always | will | remember

8. at 9 am | the Prime Minister | will arrive | tomorrow morning

9. have | uniforms | in most British schools | to wear | the students

10. to his summer party | Tom | last Saturday | invited | a lot of people

11. by bus | goes | Mr Meyers | always | to work

12. watch | Bill | last Friday | new | got | for his birthday | a

13. been | wrongly | has | she | accused | of something | never

14. twice a month | Granny | Phil and Mary | visit | usually

15. dinner | never | in the evening | has | before six | Aunt Mary

16. home | wants | her children | at seven | to be | for dinner | mother

17. all the questions | correctly | could | none of the students | obviously | answer

18. in the garden | a book | mother | reads | in summer | often | in the evening

19. his sun glasses | Patrick | at Susan's party | probably | last night | forgot

20. Peter | for breakfast | reads | has | never | in the morning | the newspaper | always | but | anything | he

21. Sue | early | did not feel | yesterday | to bed | she | because | went | fine

22. in time | Nick | his alarm clock | in a hurry | as | to get | was | had stopped | to the meeting

23. the news | gently | Ann | burst | immediately | brought | bad | to her | although | into tears | he

24. do not know | the word | in the dictionary | your teacher | look it up | if | you | ask | or

25. he | to Canada | stays | four times a year | Mr Miller | with friends | on business trips | usually | when | goes

She: "Darling, how could I ever leave you?"
He: "By bus, by bike, by train, by tram, by taxi, by plane, on foot,…"

Ziele erreicht? – Challenge 1: Word Order

Put the words in brackets in the correct places.

 See 'Topics': English around the World

England, Great Britain, and the United Kingdom

Some US television networks announced the royal baby news by welcoming the arrival of the "future king of England" (today), forgetting about the rest of the UK.

Some of the biggest names in American broadcasting have overlooked the existence of the Scots, Welsh and Northern Irish. Star presenters on CBS News and ABC News referred to the baby as "the future king of England" (frequently).

But there has not been a King of England since William III – and there won't be again, unless (or until) the United Kingdom breaks into smaller pieces completely (in the 18th century).

"The political state of the Queen's home nation is the 'United Kingdom', not England, which is one region within the country along with Scotland, Wales and Northern Ireland (just)," says Robert Blackburn, a professor of constitutional law at King's College London. "The 'United Kingdom' is shorthand for the 'United Kingdom of Great Britain and Northern Ireland'."

It is a common misunderstanding in the US. The New York Times irritated many Scots when it marked Andy Murray's Wimbledon triumph with a tweet that said: "After

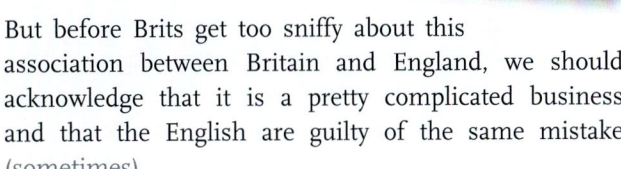

77 years, Murray and England rule" (in July).

But before Brits get too sniffy about this association between Britain and England, we should acknowledge that it is a pretty complicated business and that the English are guilty of the same mistake (sometimes).

A common error is for the British themselves to forget about Northern Ireland by referring to 'Great Britain', which is an island, when really they mean the United Kingdom.

This is a two-way street, and understanding the correct terminology connected with the US is also a tricky business. The United States of America is referred to as 'America' by British people (often), but the distinction between America and the US is important, because there is another America – Latin America, not to mention Central America and the rest of North America, including Mexico and Canada.

The answer is for everyone to be tolerant and open-minded (perhaps) … and to raise the glass in a toast to the future king.

BBC ONLINE – ADAPTED

"My wife always takes me to the pub in her car."
"Oh, does she?"
"Yes – she drives me to drink."

Ziele erreicht? – Challenge 2: Word Order

Put the words in brackets in the correct places.

 See 'Topics': Communication and the Media

Reducing screen time key to children's health

The amount of time which children spend in front of screens should be curbed to prevent development and health problems, psychologist Dr Aric Sigman says. Children of all ages are watching more screen media than ever (nowadays), and starting earlier.

He warns that the average 10-year-old has access to five different screens (at home, usually), and some are becoming addicted to them or depressed as a result. Children born today will have spent a full year glued to screens by the time they reach the age of seven.

He adds: "In addition to the main family television, a lot of very young children have their own bedroom TV along with portable hand-held computer game consoles (eg. Nintendo, Playstation, Xbox), smartphone with games, internet and video, a family computer and a laptop and/or a tablet computer (eg. iPad).

Children engage in two or more forms of screen viewing (at the same time, often), such as TV and laptop."

British teenagers are clocking up six hours of screen time a day. According to current research the negative impacts start after two hours' viewing time (already).

Dr Sigman suggests links between prolonged screen time and conditions such as heart disease, stroke and diabetes. He suggests that the effects go further than those simply associated with being sedentary for long periods. Prolonged screen time can lead to reductions in attention span because of its effects on the brain chemical dopamine (very often) which is a key component of the brain's reward system. It is connected with addictive behaviour and the inability to pay attention.

"The term 'screen addiction' is being used by physicians to describe the growing number of children engaging in screen activities in a dependent manner (frequently)," Dr Sigman says.

And there are other psychosocial problems associated with excess screen time.

These include "Facebook depression", which develops when young people spend too much time on social media sites (regularly) and then begin to exhibit classic symptoms of depression.

Dr Sigman says: "Because screen time is not a dangerous substance or a visibly risky activity (perhaps), it does not receive the attention that other health issues attract (these days).

There are many questions remaining about the precise nature of the association between screen time and adverse outcomes (still), but the advice from a growing number of both researchers and medical associations as well as government departments elsewhere is becoming crystal clear (today) – reduce screen time."

BBC ONLINE – ADAPTED

Self-Check

✓ started   ✓✓ on my way   ✓✓✓ accomplished

	✓	✓✓	✓✓✓
I can arrange the different adverbs of manner, place and time in their correct order.			
I can place the adverbs of frequency in their appropriate position.			
I can arrange all parts of a sentence in their correct order.			
I can form sentences with the appropriate word order in context.			

Literaturverzeichnis

page 8:   Coughlan, Sean: "Dark Tourism Study Centre launched by University", BBC Online, 24 Apr 2012, http://www.bbc.co.uk/news/education-17814100 (30. 10. 2013)

page 10:   O. V.: "The reality of life as a teenager in the UK and overseas", BBC Online, 23 Mar 2010, http://news.bbc.co.uk/2/mobile/school_report/8573363.stm (30. 10. 2013)

page 16:   Ross, Tim: "Research: women will be doing the housework until 2050", The Telegraph, 28 Feb 2012, http://www.telegraph.co.uk/women/mother-tongue/8526413/Researchwomen-will-be-doing-the-housework-until-2050.html (30. 10. 2013)

page 17:   Richardson, Hannah: "What can five-year-olds be expected to learn?", BBC Online, 8 Jul 2012, http://www.bbc.co.uk/news/education-23226339 (30. 10. 2013)

page 32:   O. V.: "The rise of the adult playground", BBC Online, 7 May 2012, http://www.bbc.co.uk/news/magazine-17818223 (30. 10. 2013)

page 37:   Kingsbury, Kathleen: "Degrees matter when hunting for a job", BBC Online, 7 Jun 2013, http://www.bbc.com/capital/story/20130607-is-a-degree-crucial-for-a-job (30. 10. 2013)

page 38:   O. V.: "Children bringing cold chips to school for lunch", BBC Online, 25 Feb 2013, http://www.bbc.co.uk/news/education-21573630 (30. 10. 2013)

page 42:   Kingsbury, Kathleen: "Avoid getting grilled at your office picnic", part 1, BBC Online, 2 Jul 2013, http://www.bbc.com/capital/story/20130701-picnic-at-your-peril (30. 10. 2013)

page 47:   Kingsbury, Kathleen: "Avoid getting grilled at your office picnic", part 2, BBC Online, 2 Jul 2013, http://www.bbc.com/capital/story/20130701-picnic-at-your-peril (30. 10. 2013)

page 48:   O. V.: "Web addicts withdrawal symptoms similar to drug users", BBC Online, 19 Jun 2013, http://www.bbc.co.uk/news/ukwales-22966536 (30. 10. 2013)

page 50:   Hammond, Claudia: "Shisha pipes: Is smoking them really harmless?", BBC Online, 3 Apr 2012, http://www.bbc.com/future/story/20120403-smoking-hubble-bubble-isharmless (30. 10. 2013)

page 54:   O. V.: "The role of the Royal Family", https://www.royal.uk/role-royal-family (3. 3. 2020)

page 59:   O. V.: "The reality of life as a teenager in the UK and overseas", BBC Online, 23 Mar 2010, http://news.bbc.co.uk/2/mobile/school_report/8573363.stm (30. 10. 2013)

page 60:   O. V.: "Northern: Passenger reaction to rail firm being nationalised", BBC Online, 29 Jan 2020, https://www.bbc.com/news/uk-england-51297655 (3. 3. 2020)

page 65:   O. V.: "The reality of life as a teenager in the UK and overseas", BBC Online, 23 Mar 2010, http://news.bbc.co.uk/2/mobile/school_report/8573363.stm (30. 10. 2013)

page 75:   O. V.: "Irish bid to turn Buckingham Palace green", BBC Online, 14 Feb 2013, http://www.bbc.co.uk/news/uk-northernireland-21451740 (30. 10. 2013)

page 76:   O. V.: "Scotland achieves Fair Trade Nation status", BBC Online, 25 Feb 2013, http://www.bbc.co.uk/news/uk-scotland-21571772 (30. 10. 2013)

page 79:   Murray, Janet: "Do we value vocational skills?", Guardian Online, 1 Aug 2011, http://www.theguardian.com/education/2011/aug/01/vocational-skills-vs-university (30. 10. 2013)

page 80:   McGrath, Matt: "'Extreme and unusual' climate trends continue after record 2016", BBC Online, 21 Mar 2017, https://www.bbc.com/news/science-environment-39329304 (3. 3. 2020)

page 83:   Geoghegan, Tom: "Royal baby: The American mistake", BBC Online, 23 Jul 2013, http://www.bbc.co.uk/news/blogs-magazinemonitor-23423784 (30. 10. 2013)

page 84:   Richardson, Hannah: "Limit children's screen time, expert urges", BBC Online, 9 Oct 2012, http://www.bbc.co.uk/news/education-19870199 (30. 10. 2013)

Anmerkung: Die ursprünglichen Titel der Übungstexte wurden aus pädagogischen Überlegungen in diesem Workbook abgeändert. Die Originaltitel sind im Literaturverzeichnis zu finden.

O. V. = ohne Verfasser

Literaturnachweis Witze:

Angelika Feilhauer, Cornell Ehrhardt (Hg.): Englisch lernen mit Witzen, Ravensburger Taschenbuch 1987

Bildnachweis

Notes